Inspiring Stories

for Young Women

About Hope, Strength,

and Wisdom

A FIRESIDE BOOK
Published by Simon & Schuster
New York London Toronto Sydney Singapore

CHOCOLATE

for a

TEEN'S SPIRIT

KAY ALLENBAUGH

FIRESIDE
Rockefeller Center
1230 Avenue of the Americas
New York, NY 10020

For information regarding special discounts for bulk purchases, please contact
Simon & Schuster Special Sales at 1-800-456-6798 or
business@simonandschuster.com

Manufactured in the United States of America

1   3   5   7   9   10   8   6   4   2

Library of Congress Cataloging-in-Publication Data is available.

ISBN 0-7432-2289-X

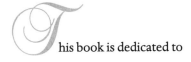his book is dedicated to

all young women who wish to learn and grow

and nurture their spirit.

May you find the faith you seek in yourself and in others.

CONTENTS

III

GROWING FROM THE INSIDE OUT

IV

BRINGING SPIRIT TO LIFE

V

TEEN MISCHIEF

VI

FROM SHIFTING SAND TO

SOLID GROUND

VII

YOU ARE NEVER ALONE

VIII

PROUD MAMAS

CHOCOLATE
for a
TEEN'S
SPIRIT

INTRODUCTION

Heartwarming, haunting, and often hilarious, the delicious true-life stories in *Chocolate for a Teen's Spirit* will remind you how much you have in common with young women everywhere. The Chocolate storytellers have shared their own moving experiences—about setting a goal and reaching it, about being the victim of a cruel trick and rising above it, about finding love in unexpected places, and about finding the divine in all things. These stories will comfort you and show you that joy often lies just on the other side of pain. You'll also discover why a bit of mischief can sometimes open the path to spiritual fulfillment.

Alive with humor, honesty, and the intimacy of close friends, *Chocolate for a Teen's Spirit* will help you discover all the facets of a spirit-filled life—ways to nurture your faith in yourself, to use your creative gifts, to find love through friends, parents, partners, and teachers, and to experience pure joy.

The stories in *Chocolate for a Teen's Spirit* are written by teens themselves as well as by women with good memories for those years gone by. From lighthearted vignettes to poignant confessions, these stories touch on the things all young women face as they move into adulthood and search for spiritual grounding during times both tame and turbulent. These stories also celebrate the mentors that I believe God supplies each of us—the role models, teachers, and friends we encounter along the way to help guide us when we're lost, believe in us when we're afraid to believe in ourselves, and cheer for us when we succeed.

So find a comfy, sacred place, nibble on some chocolate, and let the heartwarming stories in *Chocolate for a Teen's Spirit* fill your heart. As you turn the pages, listen for the messages that were meant just for you and look for the stories that would bring your friends the comfort they need as well. I hope that these stories will provide inspiration and show you how far you've come as you decide what you value, what qualities you hold dear in yourself and others, and where to find spiritual comfort when you need it most.

May *Chocolate for a Teen's Spirit* warm your heart and bring you the hope, strength, and wisdom you so richly deserve.

I

I GOTTA GET OUT OF HERE

Perspective—what made you cry at the age of six

is unimportant at 26.

Add 20 years to your evaluation of problems and chuckle.

JENNIFER JAMES

THE LOVE LETTER

Dear Billy,

I am writing to tell you goodbye. I will miss you so much. I think about you all the time, from the moment I wake up in the morning until I put the cat out at night. As soon as I fall asleep, you slip into my dreams, take me in your arms, and dance with me all night long! I wish I could be in your real arms and could feel the touch of your lips on mine. I will love you until the day I die! Even if I never see you again, I will always feel this way about you! You are the love of my life!

I signed the letter "Lots of Love, Kathy," drew a bunch of Xs and Os on the bottom, and then misted the envelope with plenty of perfume. A couple of tears on my name would have been a nice touch, but as hard as I tried, I couldn't squeeze any out. The fountain was dry; I was all out of tears. I held the letter up in front of me and admired my work. This was good stuff, but darn, something was missing. Of course! I quickly hid the letter under my pillow, slipped out of my room, checking to be sure Mom was still in the kitchen, and then sneaked into her bedroom. I opened a dresser drawer, selected the reddest lipstick I could find, smeared it all over my lips, and then tiptoed back to my room.

My hands were trembling as I pressed my red, red lips to the bottom of the letter as hard as I could. I sealed it and added another big kiss over Billy's name on the envelope, holding my lips there for the longest time. The letter was ready. Now all that remained to be done was to call my best friend Nicky and arrange for her to pick it up after church the next day.

Our family was leaving on Monday. My father had come home three weeks before and had announced that he was taking a new job in a different town. We were leaving Whittier, California, and would be moving several hundred miles away.

"*No!* Dad, *no!*" I had shouted, barely holding back the tears. "*We can't move!*"

"Why not?" Dad asked, visibly shaken by the violence of my response.

" 'Cause I don't *want* to move!"

"That's not a good reason!"

"But I won't know anybody!" I whined. I couldn't tell my father that the reason I didn't want to move was that I was madly in love with Billy Baker. If we left, I'd never see him again and then I wouldn't be able to marry him someday and have his children and live happily ever after. I knew that this wasn't the best argument for a fourteen-year-old to use on her dad, especially when he still considered her his little girl.

"Kathy, we're going to a small town. You'll make friends in no time!"

My arguments weren't working. The situation called for a smarter strategy.

"But Dad," I said, lowering my voice and adopting a reasonable tone. "I'm doing so well in school now. I really like my teachers and I'm finally getting good grades."

Dad winced. I knew that I had hit a nerve and could see that he felt terrible. Unfortunately, it was too late for him to do anything about it. All the arrangements had been made and we were going to move. Period!

Nicky met me in the park after church the next day.

I handed her the letter in a larger envelope and said, "Okay, Nicky, here it is! We're leaving tomorrow morning. Wait until lunch and then give it to him."

"Okay," she said.

"Promise me you'll wait."

"Yeah, yeah, I promise."

I wanted Billy to know that I would love him forever. I had only talked to him a few times in my life, and whenever I did, I could only gawk and mumble "Hi, Billy" before sprinting away. We were in the same history class, but I never got to sit next to him. Every time the teacher rotated the seats, somehow I always ended up migrating farther toward the back of the room while he moved closer to the front. I would have given anything if she had put me next to him. She never did. This letter was my only chance to let him know how I felt. I poured my heart out in it and, to tell the truth, I had a blast doing it. I got to tremble a lot, feel my heart flutter in my chest, and heave long dramatic sighs. Naturally, I was a little embarrassed by my plan, but I knew I'd never see him again, so I figured, *Why not?* I didn't have a thing to lose.

We moved and Nicky wrote me later that she had followed my instructions. She gave him the letter at lunch and by the time classes got out that day, he had shown it to everyone in the whole school! No one talked about anything else for at least a week. I don't know whether she was teasing or not, but she said there was even a short article about it in the school newspaper!

It took me a month to get over my embarrassment. I spent two weeks wanting to die and then another two being a very unpleasant person. The only thing that gave me any consolation was that I knew, thank goodness, that I'd never have to see any of those people again, especially Billy Baker.

I was finally getting back to being my old self and was just starting to make new friends when one afternoon, my father came into the living room with my mother. They both looked so pleased.

"I've got good news," Dad announced with a satisfied smile. I know how unhappy you've been here, Kathy. Well, guess what? I was able to get my old job back. We're moving back to Whittier!"

After a stunned silence that lasted long enough for a question mark to replace the joy in my father's eyes, I managed to squeak out, "Oh, gee, Dad, that's great! I'm so happy!" I was choking on my words, but I knew that my father had made this sacrifice to please me. I couldn't possibly do what I really wanted to do, which was to throw myself on the floor, bang my head against the hardwood, and wail, *"I don't want to move!"* But we did. A few weeks later, I returned to my old school.

When I walked into the history class, the teacher welcomed me back and assigned me my new seat, right next to Billy Baker! The red lipstick kiss I had put on my letter was a pale pink compared with the color of our faces when I sat down next to him.

We both spent the rest of the semester looking at the opposite walls of the room and never again exchanged another word. Somehow, I survived and even went on to fall in love again when I met Frankie Cooper the next summer. I had thought for sure I would love Billy Baker forever, and was surprised by how fast he had turned into the world's biggest jerk! He wasn't the love of my life after all.

KATHLEEN PIMENTEL

As we went out the door, instead of saying, "Have a good time,"
Mother would say, "Have poise!" as though it were optional.
IRENE MAYER SELZNICK

LIFE'S NO DAY AT THE BEACH

W
hen I was growing up, I was lucky enough to live in a neighborhood that was made for walking. We didn't know about summer camps and organized activities. We could walk to the library and ride our bikes to a pond. On the really hot, hot days of summer, my best friend Arlene Tarlow had a mother who would take us to the ocean that was less than half an hour away.

Arlene's mother, Alice, had the most permanently blonde, set hair in our corner of the state. But she was willing to sacrifice the effects of salt and sun to take us to Devereaux Beach on the sultriest days—when it was too hot to breathe if there wasn't salt or tidal whiffs in the air. In the mornings of days like these, one of us would wake up three streets away from the other and hear that long, hot bug buzz—heat crickets, my mother used to say—cicadas. It was The Signal. Yes! A beach day.

Alice was the only mother in our neighborhood who drove. I'd call Arlene or she'd call me, and by ten we'd stirred the limeade and made the peanut-butter-and-jelly sandwiches on Wonder Bread. Arlene's mother kept a kosher house, so there could be no ham or bologna, and because she was just plain Jewish, kosher or

not, there could be no egg salad or tuna, what with the mayon-
naise and the sun. God forbid you should get food poisoning. Our
mothers would kill us if we got food poisoning, they said, especially if it was from being stupid.

So, from when we were nine to when we were thirteen, our
two- to three-kid summer camp was hosted by Arlene's mother.
We didn't know there were people who went anywhere during
the summer, people who stayed in motels or had cabins or sent
their own children off to camp—and to this day I can't imagine
caring. The Atlantic Ocean was twenty minutes away in three directions. What more could a kid want?

'Round about age eleven we wanted more. For two years we
had sat on the private side of Devereaux Beach, where you paid
for a parking sticker, where they combed out the rocks, and where
the sand was nicer. The Tarlows must have had money—a phrase
I heard sometimes at home.

The public side was good enough, my mother said, so you
shouldn't throw away your money when it's the same ocean.
Every once in a while I'd see my own Nana Beatrice on the public side of the beach. Some good boy of a son from her group of
women friends who played a vicious version of canasta called
Bagel would drop them off, and they would don enormous
black bathing suits with skirts and harnessed bras, then take
dips.

I'd see her over there, up to her plump knees, wearing a white
bathing cap . . . ear flaps up and strap dangling, splashing water
over her chest but never ever going in farther. For my grandmother, danger was everywhere.

For Arlene and me there wasn't enough danger anywhere. By
the time we were eleven we were starting to blossom, as my
mother would say. While it was true we were getting some plum-
ing in the breast department; we were also gaining general heft
that would plague us our whole lives. We had cheesy thighs, thick
waists, and I had thick cat's-eye-shaped glasses. We were not a

pretty sight in our one-piece matching gingerbread elasticized bathing suits with ruffles on the backside.

But we were full of hormones and nerve. What ever possessed us to walk on the wild side at the end of a buzzing July day can still make me red with embarrassment and pity for those two eleven-year-olds strutting their gawky behinds across the breakwater. The waves weren't challenging enough and the sandwiches were gone. One of us had forgotten the portable radio, so we decided to take a walk.

"Be careful," Alice said. "Not too far. Those cars are crazy. Be back soon. *I'll be watching.*"

We were off. And plotting. There were four guys over eighteen in open-necked army uniforms sitting on the cement wall on the public side. We wanted desperately to catch their eye and interest. Maybe even get them to talk to us. Having just seen Joanne Woodward in *The Long Hot Summer,* we figured that Southern accents were quite sexy. And we had read Pat Boone's book *'Twixt Twelve and Twenty,* which encouraged girls to act popular in order to be popular.

We pasted smiles on our sun-mottled faces, sucked in our tummies, stuck out our tops, plopped our idea of a Southern accent onto a deep New England one, and put a slow wiggle onto our big fat cans. And we talked as we passed those boys. We spun yarns about the party the night before and who we were thinking of breaking up with and what would happen if our daddies got wind of what we were doin' with these naw-thun Yankee boys. We felt positively sixteen!

We didn't notice their looks of indifference or bewilderment or downright slap-a-thigh amusement. We thought we'd impressed the bejammers out of them. Until Nana Beatrice, back on the sand from a bit of a splash, hollered out, "Bevinka! Sha! Get away from there. You've got no shoes on that hot cement. What's the matter with you? Come down here and give your nana a kiss like a good girl."

My head went down. I tried to keep babbling, but I wasn't a very good actress then, and I gave in, shoulders sagging. I plodded over to my immigrant grandmother, dragging Arlene behind me, found out and definitely eleven again.

BEVERLY C. LUCEY

PARKING PROBLEMS

*V*alentine's Day held lots of promises when I was fifteen. After going steady with my boyfriend, Terry, for close to a year, I got permission from Mom to go out on a car date with him.

The date started off innocently enough. We ate a delicious dinner while laughing and talking with friends. After a couple of hours, Terry said that we had better leave a little early. *What a gentleman!* I thought. He seemed concerned about getting me home before my curfew. But Terry had other things on his Kentucky teenage mind.

While driving back toward my house, Terry kept hinting about the extra time we had. Since we were already on a country highway, he thought there would be no harm in stopping somewhere that was nice and quiet.

Terry turned onto an isolated gravel road that looked as if it was scarcely traveled, and he stopped the car. We decided we shouldn't let the time get away without sharing a few harmless kisses. So that's exactly what we did!

All of a sudden a loud horn blast disintegrated our romantic setting. Craning our necks to see, Terry and I were shocked to find two women in a car honking at us from behind.

Terry started the engine and began to drive down the gravel road in the opposite direction from where we'd come. I wondered why he just didn't push the gas pedal to the floor and get us out of there! But he'd just washed his car, and he didn't want our parents—especially my mother—to get suspicious, so he had to drive slowly to keep mud from splattering the car.

Terry was torn between watching out for mud-filled potholes and keeping his eye on the approaching car in the rearview mirror. What was I doing? What I always do in embarrassing situations! I began to laugh. I was afraid the ladies might know my mother, so I ducked my head and scrunched low in the seat.

Terry finally spotted a driveway on the left side of the road. Slowing the car to a halt, he examined the drive, thinking he could pull in and turn around. But it was hopeless! The car would have sunk in three feet of mud, so he kept driving deeper down the isolated road.

By that time, the two women had caught up with us, and as they pulled alongside of us, we could see the whites of their eyes. My nerves got the best of me, and I exploded into another fit of laughter. I'm sure Terry wanted to strangle me, but he was too busy dodging the foot-deep potholes and the car next to him.

Terry pulled ahead of the other car again. After a few minutes, he spotted a house on a hill and mumbled that he thought he could turn around in there. Terry breathed a sigh of relief as he pulled into the drive. We both jumped when we heard another horn blast and noticed that the car behind us wanted to turn in here, too. It seems we had actually escorted the women four miles up an isolated road to their home when Terry had been doing everything in his power to get away from them!

Feeling like an idiot, he turned around and politely waved at the two women as he squeezed his car back onto the road. I was no help at all. I just couldn't stop giggling.

We made a quick trip through the car wash, and hoped we'd get home before my curfew. As we climbed up my porch steps, our hearts raced. We walked into the house and saw my mother sitting in the living room.

"I hope you two had fun," she said. "Beautiful night for a drive, don't you think?"

Terry's face turned crimson, and he hesitated a little before agreeing with her.

And me? I wondered about a couple of things. Was this a "sign" that I wasn't supposed to be parking? And was there something else besides casual conversation behind my mother's comment as she smiled with that know-it-all twinkle in her eyes? No way! She couldn't know of our parking problems . . . or, could she?

STEPHANIE RAY BROWN

It isn't the great big pleasures that count the most;
it's making a great deal out of the little ones.
JEAN WEBSTER

HAUNTING OF HATCHET HOLLOW

It wasn't until I was sixteen that I had my first real date. Billy Granger, a popular football player, had been flirting up a storm with me at school for weeks, and he finally asked me out.

Living in Tullahoma, a small town in Tennessee, we either went to a movie or drove around, so when Billy came to pick me up, he gave me my choice. I picked riding around because Billy had a *really* cool Camaro.

By eight o'clock, we had hit all the popular hangouts—the Big K parking lot, Merle's Pizza, even the dreaded bowling alley—and I remarked, "I wish there were something exciting to do in this town."

"Oh, I know something exciting," said Billy, "but it's probably too scary for you."

"What?" I said. "Where?"

Billy stayed silent and I slid over next to him.

He spoke, but with hesitation. "Well . . . we're headed that way but . . . ever been to Hatchet Hollow?"

"Where's that?"

"It's a *real* spooky place," he said, "haunted by a real, live ghost."

"I'm not scared," I said, sort of lying. Billy was famous for teasing, and I didn't know whether or not to take him seriously. Reading my mind, he spoke up again.

"I'm serious," he said, "I've heard the ghost myself—oh, it's an awful sound! . . . Maybe we shouldn't go—"

"Yes!" I urged him. "I want to hear it! You'll protect me, won't you?" And I leaned over and gave him a kiss on the cheek.

We were driving down the Old Lynchburg Highway, way out in the county where I'd never been before. After driving about five miles, Billy made a left turn onto an old, one-lane gravel road. As we wove our way back into the wilds, he relayed the story.

"Back before even old Jack Daniel himself came to these parts, there lived a beautiful girl in the woods. Her name was Adelaide Spencer and her daddy was a preacher. Adelaide was the most beautiful girl in these parts but she was real picky about her beaus. When Adelaide was about eighteen, along came this blacksmith to town named Brighty Morgan. He came over here to set up his own smithing place near Lynchburg. The first day he was open for business, Miss Adelaide shows up with a horse of her daddy's for Brighty to shoe. They took to each other like ice cream to apple pie and soon they were seen all over town together. Brighty was real smitten with Miss Adelaide, but he was a sorely jealous young man. That turned out to be his downfall."

"How?" I said.

"Well, Brighty finally talked Miss Adelaide into getting hitched. Her daddy threw a big party the day of their wedding and folks came from all around. Adelaide looked so beautiful and Brighty was happier than a coon dog with a possum. But then everything went bad. At the end of the party, Brighty and some other guys were having a hatchet-throwing contest when Brighty spotted this fancy-dressed fellow riding toward the preacher's house on a big white horse. Then he saw Adelaide running to the fellow, and as the stranger got down off his mount, Adelaide embraced him and kissed him. Well, Brighty was furious and before he could even think straight, he threw his hatchet right at the fellow. The fellow turned and Brighty's hatchet hit Adelaide smack dab in her back. Killed her dead on the spot."

"No! And on her wedding day!" I said. "That's so *terrible!*"

"Yup," Billy went on, "and that stranger was just an uncle Adelaide hadn't seen in years. A sad story, for sure. But Brighty couldn't take it back so he ran. Adelaide's daddy rounded up a mob and they went looking for Brighty. They found him right in this hollow. Rumor has it he was beheaded."

My heart kind of leapt up into my throat and I scooted over *real* close to Billy.

"You're scared, aren't you?" he said, and he put his arm around me protectively.

"Maybe just a little," I answered.

He began to roll down the driver's window. "Just wait until you hear the ghost," he whispered loudly, "and *then* see how scared you are."

As the window went down, I hid my eyes but I *could* hear the ghost! Out in the cool night and from way down in the hollow came the chilling sound of a hatchet being hit against a tree stump. *Shhhwomp tic . . . shhhwomp tic!* Oh my gosh, it was awful!

I threw my arms around Billy's neck and suddenly he kissed me! It was *such* the right thing to do, and I momentarily forgot about being so scared.

The next night, I wanted my dad to go out there with me to hear that eerie sound. I wanted to scare him, too. But Daddy suggested we go during the day because "a ghost haunts a place all the time, not just at night." So we drove out to Hatchet Hollow on a sunny Monday afternoon.

Sure enough, Daddy was right: we could hear the same eerie sound, *shhhwomp tic . . . schhhwomp tic.*

"Come on," Daddy said, "let's go down there and investigate."

"Daddy, wait!" I said. "We'll be killed!"

"Nonsense," he said, "a ghost haunts places, not people. Besides, I won't let any ghost hurt *my* little girl."

Down the bank we went, deep down into the hollow. In a small stream at the bottom, I could see long pipes running this way and that. The sound was getting louder and Daddy motioned me to where the pipes were attached to a big water pump.

"Here's your ghost," he said, smiling. "It's just this old pump you heard pumping the water out of the stream and then resetting itself."

I had really thought a ghost lived in that dark hollow, but it was just Billy Granger using an old pump to get himself a kiss! Riding back to the house, I sat silent. My dad would laugh every now and then, but I knew he wasn't making fun of me.

When I saw Billy at school the next day, he asked me out again for Saturday night, and I agreed. I told him I wanted to hear that ghost again. He smiled as we headed down the highway to that narrow gravel road on our second date. We pulled up and parked and Billy put an arm around me. "Let's get out and walk a little," I suggested.

"Are you sure you want to do that?" he asked. "The ghost might come up out the hollow and *get us!*" And he sort of jerked me as he said it.

I made a little shriek, snuggled even closer to him, and said, "But you'll protect me, won't you?"

Billy grinned real big and we got out of his car. As soon as we shut the door, we heard a *terrible* moaning and groaning coming from down in the hollow. I jumped close to Billy and held on tight.

"Billy, I'm scared!" I said and I could tell he was, too. Just then a *huge* dark shape rose over a crest in the hilly bank, and we could both hear a mournful cry, "*I . . . want . . . my . . . head. . . . Give . . . me . . . my . . . head!*"

It was Billy's turn to shriek. He turned white as a sheet and fainted right on the spot. I looked down at him in amazement, then I turned back to see the ghost. All I saw was my dad, hunched over with a big, dark blanket wrapped around his shoulders and a huge smile spread across his face. He winked at me and took off into the woods.

When Billy came around, he looked pretty bad. "The g-g-ghost!" he said, and began to scramble backwards on the ground.

"Oh, it's gone," I told him. "I scared it away."

He looked at me funny. "Y-You s-scared it away?"

"Sure." I said. "A ghost haunts places, not people. Billy, are you feeling okay?"

He suddenly turned from white to red and mumbled something about feeling sick to his stomach.

"Must have been that hamburger I ate for dinner," he said.

"Guess so," I told him. "Glad I had the fish."

He drove me home early that night, but unfortunately, he never asked me out again. And after I saved his life.

Men.

EMILY MOOREHEAD

I DON'T KNOW
THESE PEOPLE

*I*n the Midwest in 1943, I was thirteen and the oldest of three children. Many of our weekends were spent going places in my grandmother's 1932 Ford sedan. It meant driving all day. I used to enjoy those Sunday trips, but as a new teenager, I felt too grown-up to be traveling anywhere with my family for that long.

We called my grandmother Damsy. Most of her adventures meant driving someplace distant. Once we went to a carnival off the very beaten path, and another time, to a faraway Indian pow-wow. Then there was that big revival meeting held in the open field of a devout farmer in another county.

Trailers and small tents were clustered as far as one could see, because families stayed for the weekend. A "tent meeting" was a rowdy affair. Converts were in a blissful state as they praised the Lord in their sopping-wet clothes, a sign they had just been baptized in the water trough.

When I was thirteen, a revival meeting was not my favorite event. It was noisy and emotional, which was in complete disagreement with my imagined refinement. I was glad when they were over, because the long drive home meant stopping in a small town along the way for hamburgers and root beer, and *that,* no matter what my age, was the best part about going places with my grandmother.

Damsy decided that a picnic on the way home might be more pleasant than hamburgers in a truck stop. I agreed. Dining in the countryside seemed like something that well-bred folks might do. I could barely wait for the church service to end, just so we could eat food on a blanket.

At the revival meeting, the tent was packed with people hoping for salvation in the form of a circuit preacher. We found a place near the front so my grandmother could hear every word he proclaimed. When the singing had ended, and Damsy shouted "Hallelujah" for the fifteenth time, we were out of there. On the way home, we sought an inviting location for the outdoor meal—preferably under the spreading branches of a maple tree.

How lovely it would be.

But no such place existed. Damsy got tired of the hunt and finally settled for the next thing that came along. It was a genuine disappointment. A picnic in a hot, open field was so common. And we had to bend ourselves into disgusting positions to crawl through a barbed-wire fence in order to reach our destination. Mom removed my little sister's sheer, pink Sunday dress and hung it carefully on a post. Patty looked bizarre standing in a country field wearing nothing but her slip and patent leather shoes. I was mortified and hoped that no one had seen us. But aloof cows in another field seemed to be the only living creatures.

Mama smoothed a blanket and spread a simple picnic on the ground, then poured lemonade into paper cups. Damsy said, "I've got something special for dessert," and she produced a hefty cluster of bananas . . . a real treat. When she showed us a watermelon wrapped in a blanket to keep it cool, my brother and sister became giddy with excitement.

As Mom filled our paper cups, my sister pointed behind us and said, "That's a pretty big cow."

"Oh, no." Mom was alarmed.

The approaching creature with horns was enormous, and I froze with my sandwich poised in midair. Damsy waved her arms and shouted, *"Shoo, bull!"* But he advanced slowly. My brother dropped his lunch and escaped to the fence. My sister and I did the same, while Mom dragged the picnic-covered blanket through the dirt.

My grandmother said, "Children, get through the fence. I'll grab the food."

Damsy moved fast, but her eyes never left the bull that was snorting and pawing the earth. She ripped off a banana and threw it with force. His head lowered to butt as the second banana bounced off his forehead. The golden missiles slightly interrupted his course, which barely gave Damsy time to escape. But she used up all of our dessert to reach safety.

I was terrified but mortified. The whole event was quite embarrassing. I prayed that no one in the whole wide world had witnessed my family's unrefined behavior. If they had, I planned to pretend that I was just passing by and had merely stopped to offer my help.

By then we were safely outside of the fence, and the animal was furious. He snorted bull snot everywhere. That's when I saw my sister's good Sunday dress still hanging on the post—very close to that beast.

Damsy said, "Leave it be."

"I can't," Mom said. "I paid $3.98 for that dress." And she was already trying to reach it. I was too scared to look and covered my eyes. Mama said, "Uh-oh!" I looked up to see the garment slip from her grasp on the wrong side of the fence. The raging creature attacked the pink fluff as my little sister watched in horror. The bull stomped her Sunday dress into the ground and killed it.

Patty's tears were . . . hard to describe.

There was nothing left to do but to pack up and drive home. We ate sandwiches in the car and spilled lemonade on the back seat. My sister sat half-naked between us, and I dreaded that somebody would see her like that. If they had, I would have pretended that my family was a just a group of generous strangers who had given me a lift.

I was sullen all the way home, knowing that, at thirteen, I was too old for family outings.

Damsy tried to bolster my spirits and promised, "Betty, I'll make it up to you at our very next picnic.

That's what I was afraid of.

BETTY AUCHARD

HOW SLICK STAN LEARNED PROBABILITY

*A*t exactly 1:57 *P.M.*, slam! *twenty-nine books hit* the classroom floor in precise unison. Another one of Stanley McGuillicutti's pranks had been flawlessly executed. Almost, that is. You see, there were three of us who actually cared to learn: me, Brian, the boy I secretly liked since first grade; and My-My, the Vietnamese girl who sat in front of me. Together, we would look up formulas and work through example math problems until we figured out the steps.

We worked diligently with the goal of getting out of the bonehead math class and getting in with the brainy kids who would amount to something. We three never took part in those corny conspiracies. We already resented Stan and his groupies for their pranks, which may have caused our elderly teacher, Mr. Trotter, to have a stroke. We didn't know that for sure, but we figured they had something to do with it.

Now we were faced with a substitute who didn't know a yardstick from a ruler. We would never get out of the bonehead class at this rate. While the other kids hid the teacher's edition and the chalk, the three eager bookworms stood out like a flaming red zit.

One day, that red zit must have come to a head. Good old Stan came up to me in his cheesy, sly way. Positioning himself squarely in front of me, he made suggestive, lewd comments. I told him to take a hike, and I proceeded to solve for X. In his relentless way, he attempted to land an insult before returning to his seat. "At least I don't stuff my bra," he said loudly.

"Stanley, I never knew you wore a bra."

At that point, the substitute called me to her desk to explain what had taken place. I returned to my seat just before the bell rang. I tried to get up but couldn't. Sneaky Stanley had poured rubber cement on my chair. Of course, he lingered behind just long enough to relish the moment and witness my embarrassment.

As fate would have it, I am a teacher now. I love to teach pre-algebra and probability. I see the Stanleys and the My-Mys and the Brians and the groupies. But when I see them, I see the road beyond the grimy desk, the heavy backpack, and the notorious class clown. It is likely they will all learn a lesson of probability and balanced equations some day. I know I did. I didn't allow the groupies to keep me from working hard, dreaming, and succeeding.

That very tough year I got on the honor roll. Stanley got expelled. He is selling cars now. I know that because I saw him when I was proudly looking for a car when my career was finally in order. I wouldn't have known him, except that I recognized his big mouth. He insisted that I looked familiar. He was no doubt hoping to make a sale to one of his former groupies.

Initially, I brushed him off, informing him I never went to Cappuccinos High or any of the other schools he mentioned. Finally, I told him that I went to school out of state, and I had gone to Borel Middle School for two years before I moved away. He told me he'd gone to Borel for a while before he got kicked out.

"So what's your name?" I asked, even though I already knew.

"Stanley McGuillicutti."

"Yes, I know you," I sighed.

"I thought so!" he beamed.

"We had math together. You put rubber cement on my chair, remember that? That was charming," I said sarcastically.

From Stanley came a humble, unforgettable stammer: "I did a lot of childish things back then. Now, um, about the car . . ."

Confidently, I dropped the keys he had given me back into his hand. Nothing more needed to be said. The equation had been balanced.

LAURIE NUCK

II
DISCOVERING LIFE'S TREASURES

Once we are willing to accept that anything worth doing might even be worth doing badly, our options widen.

JULIA CAMERON

YOU CAN'T GO BACK

Johnny smelled like leather. Not just from the Shawnee High School football jacket he wore all of our junior year in Oklahoma, but his skin literally reeked of that delicious scent.

I leaned my head on his shoulder one evening as we sat in front of my house on Park Street during the last week of our school term. We looked through the windshield of his old Ford pickup, marveling at the bright sky covering our small town like a protective veil.

"That's our moon," he said. "Our moon is big and full, just like our future."

It was something he'd said before, lots of times, but I still agreed, "Um-hum."

That's how it was. Our future lit up like the moon, reflecting life's bright promises. We'd been going steady for two years. I never missed one of his football games. We ate lunch together on the school's front lawn. He helped me with math while I deciphered his poetry homework. We shared sock hops, Tri-Hi-Y fundraisers, church teen gatherings, pep-club rallies, and foot-long hot dogs at the drive-in on Harrison Street. Photographs of our history had filled the friendly pages of our school newsletter like clockwork. Van's Bar-B-Q even lacquered their new tables with our shared events.

"Oops, ten o'clock," he said, running his long fingers through my short, sandy-colored hair as I turned to meet his blue-eyed gaze head on. We leaned in toward each other for our good-night kiss. My heart fluttered as our lips met. I melted, willingly, into his magnetic energy.

We had kissed each other earlier in the evening, but something about the last kiss always created a deeper connection. It was a seal left to encase our love until we could meet again.

My dreamlike feelings were swept away as soon as I walked into the door of my house. I knew something was wrong, but I didn't know what it was. The air was heavy, making it hard to breathe. My parents sat at opposite ends of the living room sofa, coffee cups in hand, looking ashen and staring into space.

My first concern was for my brothers. Jim had just gotten his driver's license. *Maybe he had an accident,* I thought.

"Jim okay?" I asked quickly.

They nodded affirmatively.

"Butchie?" At thirteen, he was too young to drive, but that didn't stop him from stumbling into trouble on a footpath.

"Yes, he's fine," they mumbled.

Since my brothers were okay, the only solution to the pain on my parents' faces had to be me. I stood ready to apologize, but I just couldn't figure out what I could have done.

Finally, I gave up and asked, "You mad at me for something I don't know about?"

"No," Momma answered, shaking her head back and forth, her long brown hair swinging from side to side.

Relief that it wasn't me didn't change the gloom still lying all around us, but I didn't know what else to do, so I turned to go to my room and get ready for bed. That's when it hit me. Somebody must have died. That was the only thing I hadn't questioned.

I turned back and gently asked, "Somebody I don't know about die?"

My father looked over at my mother, put his coffee cup on the table next to him, cleared his throat, and said, "We're moving."

"Across town?" I queried, still not sure why their faces were so drawn, or maybe not wanting to know.

"To another state," Momma answered hesitantly.

"We can't," I protested, thinking they must have gone mad. Moving seemed the worst option of all. Worse than anyone getting sick, breaking a leg, or even dying. It meant ripping away everything I'd come to know—everything that helped to define who I was.

"What'll I do? My whole future is here. I'm going into my senior year. I'm captain of the pep team, teaching dance at the academy, all my friends are here, and . . . what about Johnny? We're . . . *soul mates,"* I shouted desperately, trying to get them to see my side of the story.

It didn't work. My words fell on deaf ears. They just sat there looking glum but not giving an inch. My life was over. I ran to my room, slammed the door, and fell on my bed crying.

We moved the next week. Momma wanted to set up house before the next school term in a place that was as unfamiliar to her as it was to my brothers and me. I thought I had the most nonunderstanding parents in the world. *If they loved me, they wouldn't have moved.* I sulked for days, sure that they wanted to punish me for something. Then I found out why we had to leave.

My father had lost his job. The small town we were in was great for kids. It gave us a safe place to roam the streets, discover the countryside, and spend time together in so many wonderful ways. But it didn't allow the same opportunities for adults. There weren't very many jobs. Moving was the only option. Dallas was a big city. An engineering firm had hired him.

Johnny and I wrote each other and telephoned on Sundays month after month. When my parents had to relocate again, seven months later, I excitedly moved back to that small town to finish my senior year. The gracious family of a friend made room for me.

It was harder coming back than I thought. Half of the semester was gone. I was behind in some classes and ahead in others. Friends had filled in my vacancy with other friends. Even Johnny didn't have as much time for me as he did before.

"We can't go to the dance Saturday," he explained. "I have to figure out plays for the next football game."

One excuse for missing dates led to another. He had to fix his truck . . . build a fence . . . paint his room.

The lunch hour we usually shared became sporadic. He had to study math with Kent, physics with Richard, or English with Carol. Not poetry with me.

"She's just an old friend," he said after I saw him walking hand in hand down the hall with Carol.

"Friends don't look at each other like you two do," I said huffily.

We began to argue a lot. Since I was alone, without my family, I needed more of him than he did of me. I felt unsure of my future and of myself.

Johnny was going to go to a university to study engineering. I couldn't afford to go to school right away. I had to work first.

We said goodbye again at the end of our senior year. My father found a job for me in Ohio. That's where my family had relocated. Again, Johnny and I promised to write, call, stay in touch. But it just wasn't the same. While Johnny went off to college with his friends, I worked in an office in a city of strangers from nine to five. When he finished his first year of studies, I went to New York to take up a dance career. Our connection didn't survive life's changes.

As my first love, Johnny will be a part of me for the rest of my life, yet I've learned that it rarely works to go back. I know that wherever I land there'll be a moon. Once a month, it'll be big enough to light up the whole sky. Instead of going back, going forward now fills my heart with anticipation—because who knows what great adventure the next move will bring.

JUDITH MORTON FRASER

He's a Taco Bell, Domino's Pizza type of guy; that's why I love him.
JENNIFER ANISTON

NOT MY TYPE

"**S**o would you go on a date with him if he asked?" Tammy was trying to fix me up with a friend of her boyfriend's. That must be why she coaxed me into going bowling with her.

"He's not my type," I said, as I looked at him again. It was obviously not the first time he had worn that faded concert T-shirt bearing the name of a group unfamiliar to me. His faux-leather belt was cinched tightly around his bony waist, gathering the fabric of his worn jeans. His bowling shoes were the only part of his outfit that looked new. They weren't the alley rentals that most people were wearing; his were all one color—the mark of a frequent bowler.

No, he wasn't at all the type of guy I was attracted to. I preferred the muscular, athletic type. My ideal guy would dress in khakis and button-down shirts. He would never own a bowling ball.

"Well, why don't you give him your number anyway?" she said, interrupting my thoughts.

Good point, I told myself. *Why not?* I had planned to spend most of my summer college break hanging out with Tammy, but that was before her boyfriend proposed and they started spending all of their time making wedding plans. Since I was going to have nothing to do all summer, why not go on a date with "Bowler Bob"? It would be a free meal, maybe a movie. The altruistic side of me wanted to help boost this poor guy's self-esteem. What could it hurt?

"Okay," I said, "I'll give him my number if he asks."

She went over and told him. I felt like I was back in seventh grade with my best friend telling some boy, "Lisa likes you. Do you like her?" What a loser I must be. Why did I agree to this? Ah, yes, I felt sorry for him. It would be a pity date.

Although he was supposedly interested in me, he didn't talk to me the entire evening. *He's either the strong silent type, or painfully shy,* I thought. Taking another look at him, I knew it must be the latter. Maybe he's too shy to ask for my number, I hoped.

When the time came to leave, I got up to pay for the games I had bowled. He stood, too, and very awkwardly approached me.

"May I have your phone number?" his voice trembled as sweat formed on his brow.

Darn, I thought, *I was so close.* "Sure," is what he heard me say.

He smiled broadly as I dictated the number. "I'll call you. Maybe we could go out next weekend."

"Yeah, maybe," I said, and I headed out the door.

He didn't call the following day, or the next. At first I was relieved. Then I got irritated. As the days continued to pass without his call, I became angry. I only agreed to go out with him so he wouldn't feel bad. How dare he not call!

Six days later I answered the phone and heard his voice. "So do you want to get together tomorrow?" he asked.

"That'd be fine," I replied, completely surprised by my response. These were not the words I had planned to say if he called. "What do you want to do?"

"I was thinking maybe dinner and a movie. Can I pick you up at seven?"

"Sure."

He arrived a few minutes late the next evening, flowers in hand, and knocked at the door. My father went outside, informed him that the door he was rapping on was to our detached garage, and escorted him to our house. I was relieved to see that he was not wearing his bowling shoes, though they may have been more stylish than the orthopedic-looking pair he'd donned. Other than that, he looked nice, in gray pants and a green-and-black striped shirt. Not what my dream guy would have chosen for our first date, but it would suffice.

I was still apprehensive about the whole arrangement, but as I climbed into his car—a huge maroon hand-me-down from his grandfather—I convinced myself to just go and have fun.

And, surprisingly, I did have fun. In fact, it was the best date I had ever been on. After an initial awkwardness, we started talking and didn't stop. He was funny and interesting, and we had a lot in common. I felt an unusual connection between us, and I was disappointed when the evening ended.

He called the next day and thanked me for the date. And just as I was hoping he would, he asked for another . . . and then another. Before we knew it, three years had passed. He suggested that we spend every evening together for the rest of our lives. I joyfully agreed.

Eleven years ago I dated a guy who was not my type. Eight years ago I married my perfect match. Sometimes I still can't believe it's the same man. He is not what I had imagined; he is better than any childhood fantasy. My dream guy may be out there somewhere, but my soul mate is right here.

LISA SANDERS

KAY'S TIPS FOR TEENS

1. You can often create a better ending to something that didn't have a great start.
2. If you question why you are here, know that God has something wonderful for you to do.
3. Look outside today and notice all the beauty—no matter where you are.
4. Reach out each week to a different person that you don't know well and get to know him or her better. This will bring richness to you both.
5. Guys marry women they respect. Be a woman you would respect.
6. Pretend today is your last day alive. What would you do? Add those things to your life right now.
7. Be a hero. Have the courage to stand up for people who are being made fun of.
8. While you cannot change anyone else, you can change yourself—your thoughts, feelings, and actions.
9. Discover the wisdom of your grandparents and ask them what the most important thing is they've learned so far.
10. Make sure you have all the qualities you are seeking in someone else.
11. Be the wind beneath another person's wings.
12. Have discussions with God. He is always listening and guiding you.
13. Make yourself proud by taking responsibility for what you say and do.

14. If something doesn't go well, ask yourself, What positive thing can I learn from this experience?
15. Always remember that following behind any dark day is light.
16. Notice how upbeat music and comedy make you feel better.
17. Being kind to everyone makes you more beautiful—inside and out.
18. Take a stand for something positive that will make a difference in the lives of others.
19. Patriotism for your country will give you a sense of belonging.
20. Look at your teachers with a fresh set of eyes. Some may forever impact your life.
21. What courageous conversation are you avoiding? What deserved acknowledgment for someone else are you withholding?
22. Behind what you fear is often your greatest learning. Walk through your fears.
23. It is not the circumstances that define you; it's your choices that matter.
24. Each day, do something to nurture your spirit—and feed your soul.
25. Honor your unique strengths by giving your talents and gifts to the world.

KAY ALLENBAUGH

A GOOD LESSON

*E*nglish was one of my favorite classes in the eighth
grade. I liked everything about it: grammar, reading, and
especially the writing assignments.

Miss Polanski announced one day, "Students, next week submit
a story about an exciting event that happened in your life." The
kids all groaned. "Well, then, if your life was that boring, invent
something. But it had better be good."

I couldn't wait to dazzle my teacher with a good tale. I started
early by making a list of hair-raising events in my life:

when my brother fell out of a second-story window
when I caught my sister's lip in a zipper
when my brother almost cremated us in our cornstalk tepee
when my uncle put me in the washing machine

My topics sounded boring, so I decided to invent a story that
was way better than anything on that list. I worked on my
creation all week long and let my imagination run wild, inserting
a little bit of action and lots of big words. I was terribly impressed
with the results, and I knew that Miss Polanski would be, too.

I was certain that if there were a Pulitzer Prize for eighth-grade
students, I would win it. I pictured the teacher's note after the A
that I would get: "Elizabeth, see me after class to discuss your
promising future as a writer."

When our assignments were due a week later, my best friend
and I were eating a "gourmet" lunch in the school cafeteria. Suddenly, Shirley interrupted her chewing, slapped her forehead, and
exclaimed, *"Oh, no!* I forgot to write my story!"

Half-eaten fish sticks muffled her words, but I got the gist of it and jumped to her rescue. "Shirley, I'll write your story. We've got a whole half hour before the class starts."

She finished chewing, swallowed hard, and accepted my offer.

There wasn't time to weigh my choices. I grabbed something from my head and slammed it onto paper. I felt exhilarated after belting out words that had rescued my best friend, and we laughed all through the day about our noontime writing frenzy. On the way home from school, Shirley joked, "Lizzie, wouldn't it be funny if I got a better grade than you?"

"No," I snorted. "I don't think that would be funny at all." And we exploded into fits of laughter.

The next week I could hardly wait for our stories to be returned. I anticipated being asked to read mine to the class, but it didn't happen. Shirley's bad joke came true: She got the better grade. I was numb. I had dashed off her story in thirty minutes, and it got an A.

I got a C+.

The worst part was the note below my friend's A: "Shirley, have you ever considered writing as a career?"

I almost screamed, *"Yes, Miss Polanski—I have!"* I wanted to confess that I was the author of Shirley's adventure story.

But my best friend said, "Lizzie, I know how you feel, but think about this: We'll *both* get a failing grade if you tell."

I was as gloomy as an eighth-grade girl could be and despondent all day long. But I learned more from that experience than from any teacher. I learned never to do other people's work if they can do it for themselves. I also discovered that grueling, hard work can be good, but—amazingly enough—fast is sometimes better.

BETTY AUCHARD

If hindsight were ahead of time, we'd all be better off.
CINDY POTTER

GETTING OVER HIM

That Saturday afternoon I came back from summer camp in a complete daze. I had met an amazing guy named Ryan whom I couldn't stop thinking about. All I wanted to do was get home and wait for him to call me. Then something rather unpleasant occurred to me. I already *had* a boyfriend, and a sweet one at that. I mean, he did send me countless letters and packages while I was at camp. He was my first boyfriend, and we had been going out for eight months. That was like a record or something in our grade.

Pretty much everyone thought we were totally perfect for each other, including me. But I guess I had a spurt of insanity the day I got back from camp, because I dumped him via an e-mail that went something like this:

Dear Max,
I am sorry, but things just aren't working out between us. We aren't getting along, and I just want a break right now. I hope we can still be friends, and I'd like to consider getting back together once school starts. Hope you understand.
Always,
Anne

So of course the only thing he could do was accept the fact that I didn't want to go out with him anymore, and claim to agree with everything I said. I later realized that what he wanted was not a little break, or to just be friends, but simply to protect his pride. I guess I had a lot to learn about boys.

Summer quickly passed and school started before I knew it. I had received an occasional e-mail from Ryan, but not a single phone call. I was utterly disappointed, but soon got over him. I still liked Max (a lot) and just planned to breeze right back into school, flash him my sweet smile, dazzle him with my fresh tan, and have things be back to normal once again. We had liked each other too much to just get over each other so quickly, or so I thought. Apparently, the feeling was not mutual. He seemed to show no interest in me at all, but I still kept hope.

When our first school dance of the year rolled around, I was so excited I couldn't stand it. This was my chance to get Max back!

As it got later into the evening at the dance, one of my friends came up to me and said, "Anne, did you hear?"

"Hear what?"

"Max just asked Kathryn out! Everyone is talking about it! He thinks he's so cool because he is going out with an older girl. Can you believe it?"

I could not even reply as tears filled my eyes and I hurried into the rest room. How could he ask her out? I was so angry. Not at him, but at myself for letting him slip away as I had. It was a huge mistake to dump him in the first place and the realization of that hurt more than anything else.

I knew I had made a mistake, and immediately saw how crazy I had been to leave Max for a guy I hardly knew or had true feelings for. So I composed myself, walked back into the gym, and somehow managed to get through the evening, trying to act as if it were not bothering me at all.

For the whole school year, I felt the same way. I knew it was sort of unhealthy to be so hung up on him, but I felt like I was in love with him and could never move on. Something about him being my first boyfriend really affected my perspective, and I could never quite comprehend how he had gotten over me so quickly. Maybe it's better that I never figured it out, because I know that the answer would probably just have caused me more pain than I could handle.

Every day I would hope for two things—that either Max would break up with the girl he was currently going out with, or I would have an incredible revelation and suddenly be over him.

Max and Kathryn eventually broke up, yet Max and I never ended up back together. I literally hoped and prayed every night that something would change his mind about me, and fell asleep dreaming about the various ways he might apologize and try to win me back, but it was all in vain.

To this day, I still regret my decision and can't help but wonder what would have happened if only I had realized how important Max was to me. Despite the numerous times I replay the whole thing in my mind (or maybe it's my heart), I always come back to the same conclusion: It could be different. I could have kept all of this from happening, but I made a stupid mistake that cost me a year of tears, suffering, and total heartache.

Even though I am not over the boy, I have realized the situation is out of my hands. Being older, and I hope a bit wiser, I've come to learn how important it is to stop and think through the decisions I make. I let go of Max so quickly—on a whim really—and have regretted it ever since. It's ironic that I now know how to take care of my special relationships—something that Max deserved all along.

ANNE PENNEBAKER

WORTH WAITING FOR

I *am twenty-eight years old and I am single. I haven't* dated anyone seriously in (should I really admit this out loud?) an entire year. I am solo. Swinging single. On the go. I'm a busy career gal with a plan of action. My friends are getting married and having babies. Some are getting divorced. I am living the high life, supporting myself, making a good living, traveling, and yes, feeling lonely. According to my little sister Kate, who turns thirteen this year, my standards are too high.

"Jacque," she said one afternoon, "you're not married because you're too picky."

"I am not," I replied.

"Are too."

"Prove it," I said.

"You broke up with one guy because he wore knee-high white socks," Kate said while holding up a finger.

I shrugged and grimaced. Surely she could understand that one.

Kate held up a second finger. "You kicked that guy to the curb last summer because his lips were too thin."

"Well, they were!" I felt the beginnings of discomfort.

"He could have been a poet!" she said dramatically, her arms stretched to the heavens as though asking for the patience to continue pointing out the obvious.

A third finger went up in the air. "Another one you dumped because his voice was too nasal," she said. "And another because he had buggy eyes and was a Republican."

"What's the problem?" I asked, trying to justify my reasons for singlehood. "Just wait until you start dating, you'll see!" I declared defensively. "Besides, I'm a jet-set businesswoman who doesn't have time to date!"

Kate just shook her head and pulled out a copy of *Cosmo Girl*. She flipped it open and pointed to a chair. "Sit," she demanded. "We'll find out what's wrong with you." With pen in hand, she gave me the teen love quiz.

She asked me if I liked flowers on Valentine's Day, what I would do if I caught my boyfriend cheating on me, and how I liked my eggs in the morning, among other things. At the end she added up my points and then, with an expression of great understanding, she nodded her head and sighed. Tapping the pen on the magazine in a very businesslike and maddeningly reasonable manner, Kate explained my results.

"Here's your problem. You're too romantic," she said.

"What? That's it? I could've told you that!" I said. My cheeks flushed thinking of the piles of romance novels I'd secretly read over the years, my collection of romantic movies, my hidden belief in the existence of a Prince Charming perfectly programmed to my long list of specifications.

Like many of the girls . . . ahem . . . I mean women my age, I can now actually hear my biological clock tick-tock-ticking away in my body as thirty looms on the horizon. My list has gotten shorter, but the gems remain. He must be tall, handsome—to me at least—kind, witty, confident, motivated, and emotionally mature. Oh, and he can't wear white socks to his knees.

Kate hasn't started dating yet, but when she does, I certainly hope she knows that she can afford to take her time. She doesn't have to end up with the first man that comes along. She's worth waiting for, and so am I.

JACQUELYN B. FLETCHER

III
GROWING FROM THE INSIDE OUT

May you continue to find all the light you can hold.

SUSIE TROCCOLO

"*B*ri, *when I said he needed someone more like you, I* didn't actually mean *you.*"

I glance up nervously. "You going to hate me forever?" I ask hesitantly.

Lori gives me a skeptical stare. "Stop looking so guilty and miserable. I couldn't hate you for a week. We both know that Aaron and I never really worked. Now, you and him," she shakes her head as if still disbelieving my announcement of our hookup, "it was inevitable. I'm not mad at you. Just never tell me about how happy you are. I would have to hurt you for that."

I let out my breath and smile for the first time today. The hard part is over now. "Thanks," I say.

"Don't mention it." Lori laughs as she gives me a shove out her front door. "Go talk to your new boyfriend!"

My new boyfriend . . . Aaron. My closest guy friend, my best friend's ex-boyfriend, and my ex-boyfriend's ex-best friend—now my boyfriend. Who would have ever guessed? I close my eyes and let my mind wander back to when he and I first met a little over a year and a half ago. Neither of us gave the other much thought then. No, then my eyes were on Alex, and he was working his way toward Lori. Funny how things change. I can still remember the double dates the four of us used to take: the beach trips, the movies, the lazy summer days. It all seems so far away now.

And Alex—boy, have I grown up since him. Alex . . . I wonder what he will say when he finds out about Aaron and me? He, too, will probably say it was inevitable, yet I doubt he will take it nearly as well as Lori. Somewhere in the back of my mind I wonder if Alex still believes that he and I are destined for each other. I still believe we should never have been together in the first place.

Alex was my first official boyfriend, my first big mistake, and my first broken heart. I will never forget the day I sat meekly on the edge of my bed desperately trying to explain to him how the magic of our relationship had faded and our love had somehow turned into tolerance. I will also never forget the explosion that followed—the weeks of heated arguments, hot tears, and hurt pride.

Somewhere in that mess of postrelationship confusion I lost myself. All my confidence in my ability to love failed. I had hurt Alex so much. I had hurt myself so much. How could I ever go through that again? No, my relationship days were over. Casual dating would be fine. No commitment meant no getting hurt. Boyfriends were definitely out of the question . . . or so I thought.

We were sitting on my front porch the day Aaron asked me out. It was a late February afternoon. I sat self-consciously playing with my hair while he watched my every move with an intensity that made me blush in silent dread and anticipation.

"Bri, will you go out with me?"

It was just like that, perfectly sudden and perfectly straightforward, and it sent every carefully preplanned word flying from my mind.

"It . . . it's against the rules," I mumbled weakly, fighting down the fear and insecurity that rose in my throat. How could I say yes? I had promised myself I'd never let something like this happen. Aaron and me—no, the match would be illogical, insensible, not to mention practically illegal! Even so . . . how could I possibly tell him no, when I wanted him so badly?

Aaron laughed softly as though the battle inside me were of little consequence. "I guess that makes me a rebel," he said gently.

For the first time that afternoon I dragged my eyes up from the pavement to meet his. There, in the steady green of Aaron's eyes, as if it had always been and always would be, was the answer I had been searching for.

I shake myself out of my reverie as I pull up to Aaron's house, turning off the car and sitting back for a moment. I glance at the door. He hasn't seen me yet. Picking up my wallet, I carefully slide out the top photo and stare at it for a moment. Aaron's smiling face stares back. *Boyfriend,* I test the word, laughing as a little tingle runs down my back. It's a good word now. Aaron has taught me that. Through the bumps and turns in our friendship, the late nights of soul searching, of sharing our fears and our hopes, the countless memories of fun and laughter—somewhere, somehow, a connection was made. A connection I know I can trust. A connection that feels good.

We've come a long way, Aaron and I. But I know as I slip his picture into my back pocket and walk slowly up to his door we have a lot farther to go, and I am so glad.

BRIANNA MAHIN-AYERS

THE CHRISTMAS BALL

I had read and heard all about it, and I knew what to expect. Someday I would look like the other girls. The braces would disappear. I'd have long, straight hair, contact lenses, and breasts. In short, I was going to be beautiful, and almost as critical as my outer beauty, I'd be able to act in that bubbly, outgoing way that came with such ease to the popular girls. The books I read and the movies and TV shows I watched all promised me. As when an ugly caterpillar turns into a beautiful butterfly, the metamorphosis was guaranteed.

It didn't happen. I was fifteen years old when I entered grade twelve, and because I was younger than my classmates were, I rationalized that my transformation might take longer. I tried to be patient. My father, in an attempt to console me, called me a late bloomer. I was afraid that I would never bloom at all.

One day, my locker partner, Donna, a cheerleader with confirmed status as one of the social elite, struck up a conversation with me. I was very flattered, and when she asked if I'd be interested in going to the Christmas ball at a prestigious local military college, I was stunned. She explained that her boyfriend was a cadet at the college, and his roommate needed a date. *This has to be some kind of joke,* I thought, but Donna's sincerity convinced me to say yes. I was filled with excited apprehension. I was going on my first date.

I rushed home with my thrilling news. My mother was elated. "We'll need to find a dress, and you'll have to have your hair done," she announced. These requirements hadn't occurred to me, and I was overwhelmed with fresh worries. Where would I get a dress? Get my hair done? I'd never been to a hair stylist. Everything had to be perfect for this remarkable occasion. That night before bed, I looked in the mirror and was filled with despair. No dress or hairstyle could change the fact that the image staring back at me bore no resemblance to the girl I pictured going to the Christmas ball.

The dress came from next door. My news was shared with our neighbor, who produced her daughter's old prom dress as the perfect solution to the wardrobe dilemma. My mother rushed home so I could try the dress on. It was hideous, and unfortunately, it was a perfect fit. Why didn't I tell my mother that I hated it? I don't know. Perhaps I didn't want to spoil her obvious pleasure. I convinced myself the dress would be okay. I would get my hair done, and it would be so lovely that no one would notice my gruesome dress.

Time crawled by. An engraved invitation arrived in the mail. I had several pleasant phone conversations with my date, David, and relaxed a little, because, to my amazement, he seemed to like me.

The day of the dance arrived, and I went to my hair appointment. As I sat in the chair, I was rendered speechless with nerves, unable to tell the stylist what I wanted. Without my instructions, she took it upon herself to pile my shoulder length hair on top of my head in a ghastly arrangement of stiff, teased curls. I began to hope that a bus might hit me on the way home from the salon.

David arrived at seven, corsage in hand. My father answered the door, and brought him upstairs, where I waited in the living room. One look at David's eyes, filled with disappointment, told me that the best thing I could do would be to tell him I was unable to go. My father prolonged the agony and insisted on taking pictures.

Finally, we left the house and made our way to the car. Donna and her date were in the back seat. A smile quivered on Donna's lips. "You look lovely," she said. *You liar,* I thought, and resisted the temptation to open the door and run back inside.

The evening was a nightmare. David fulfilled his obligation, and danced with me once or twice, but for the most part, I spent the evening in the corner, praying for invisibility. At the end of the night, he accompanied me to the door, pecked me on the cheek, and said, "Thanks." I never saw him again. Of course, my mother was waiting up. I held back the tears and told her I had a wonderful time. Wearing a satisfied smile, she went to bed.

The next day at school, all the girls who attended the ball were engaged in excited gossip. I made an effort to join in, but their responses and attitudes told me I was still an outsider. Later that day, I was approached by a girl named Lori. "I just thought you should know," she said, "that your date won the prize." I was confused. "The prize?" A smirk appeared on her face. "Yes. Every year all of the cadets put a quarter in the pot, and the guy with the ugliest date wins the money." She laughed and walked away. I was devastated.

I relived every horrible minute of that evening over and over again. Instead of the acceptance I had hoped to gain, I was still an outsider. My prayer for invisibility that night at the dance was finally answered.

I felt betrayed. The promise had not materialized. I was convinced that I would always be the girl whose date received the prize. I told myself it didn't matter, and I tucked the pain away deep in my heart. I was lucky enough to have a horse, and I immersed myself in the world of riding and showing him.

As my father predicted, I was a late bloomer. One day the braces came off and my mother took me to the eye doctor to be fitted for contact lenses. My friends from the riding stable and I experimented with makeup, and practiced the personalities we were certain would lead to success in our social lives.

To my amazement, boys began to ask me out. When they told me I was pretty, I didn't believe them. Didn't they know I had been the ugliest girl at the Christmas ball? They had to be lying. Why wasn't I happy? Then it occurred to me that nothing had changed. I was still being judged by my outward appearance. I had become the butterfly, but I was waiting for something more. I wanted someone to look beneath the surface where the real me lay hidden.

At university, and then in my career as a teacher, I began to meet people who recognized my inner as well as my outer beauty, and I believe that's when the real metamorphosis occurred. Their acknowledgment of my inward qualities made me feel truly beautiful, and when I looked in the mirror, I liked what I saw. I met and married a man who not only fell in love with the way I looked, but was enchanted with the person inside.

The pictures my father took that night are in a drawer upstairs. When I look at them, I can still feel twinges of the humiliation, and flickers of the pain from not so many years ago. Time has given me the wisdom to be grateful that I was, and still am, the person inside that terrible dress and underneath that mountain of hair. Maybe the packaging wasn't right, but the contents were great.

SUSAN B. TOWNSEND

*You never know how an act of compassion
can change a life forever.*
MARY MANIN MORRISSEY

IN ONE FELL SWOOP

Nancy and Joan were not friends of mine. In my
everyday life, that was of no concern to me. I didn't
need Nancy and Joan to be my friends; I had plenty
of friends. I was smart and funny and cute and everyone knew
it, although many of them probably said behind my back that I
was smart-mouthed, self-centered, and boy-crazy, and that was
true, too.

My interest in Nancy and Joan changed when our teachers
chose them to be the coeditors of the yearbook. The job of yearbook editor was an honor, one I would have liked to earn for
myself. However, that issue was secondary to a more serious im-
plication. The editors of the yearbook were given the powerful
responsibility of writing one-line captions underneath the photograph of each graduating senior.

Given the small number of students in my high school, every-
body knew everyone else, and after nearly twelve years of going
to school together, we all had personal favorites—and old resent-
ments. Now, Nancy and Joan had the opportunity to put a label on
each of us without our permission or foreknowledge. Whatever
those two girls thought of any of us would be published in the

yearbook under our picture and encapsulate our lives for all gen-
erations to come.

The day the final copy of the yearbook was approved by the
English teacher and sent off to the printer, Nancy and Joan gleefully began revealing what they had written. Underneath the picture of someone they believed to be dishonest, they had written
the caption, *Truth conquers all.* For a girl who'd had, in their opinion, a few too many boyfriends they wrote, *If I knew then, what I
know now.*

"Guess what we wrote about you?" Nancy asked me in our
gym class. "A wiggle in her walk and a giggle in her talk."

Whew, I thought, *it's dopey, but at least it's not cruel.*

Four months later, two days before graduation, the yearbooks
arrived. The huge cartons from the printer were torn open, and
we eagerly rushed through the book. There I was in the senior
pictures with a caption that read, *Small package, big person.*

I was stunned. More stunned were Nancy and Joan.

"We didn't write that!" Nancy said, and she opened the folder
that contained the original copy for the yearbook—the manu-
script pages from which the printer set the book. A thin line
was drawn in red ink through *A wiggle in her walk and a giggle in her
talk,* and in the unmistakable fine, Palmer-penmanship hand of
Mrs. Walker, our English teacher, was written, *Small package, big
person.*

The serene, gracious, and wise woman whom I respected—
and feared—thought that selfish, loud, conceited, silly me was a
big person? Mrs. Walker's one-line edit of a picture caption in
a high-school yearbook forty years ago changed my life. The
change was not one hundred percent. From time to time, I have
been mean and petty and deceptive and egocentric, unkind and
unreliable, thoughtless and destructive. I have also been strong
and courageous, generous and fair, loving and loyal. A big person.
Something I didn't know I could be until someone—who was a
very big person herself—gave me the gift.

The best part? She didn't say, If you do this and that, if you work hard enough, if you're lucky, if you're very good—you can be a big person. She said, You already are.

WENDY (REID CRISP) LESTINA

My boyfriend of three years had lost his college ROTC scholarship, and when his parents said, "You have to come home," we decided I should come home too. At the time, it sounded like a good idea. Our social life at the university in Austin, Texas, had been tied to the ROTC students, and if he wasn't in the program, I didn't feel the university had much to offer us.

So we both enrolled at the smaller university in our hometown, San Antonio. He seemed to want things to go on as they did before, but something inside me wanted something different. He stayed with his business major, but since the new university didn't have a speech department, I chose to become an English major.

In Austin, we had taken many classes together. Now in our third year, we were both taking courses in our majors. We only saw each other between classes, or if we rode together in his car or mine to the university.

Besides English classes, I enrolled in a Texas history class. The professor would take roll by reading out an entire name. It was something about the way he said, "Diane Theresa Gonzales," putting in all the Spanish accents on my names, that made me feel so proud of myself as a Mexican American. That first day he called my name, he also added, "And what does a person named *Diana Teresa Gonzalez* plan to do with her life?"

At the time, I could only shrug and say, "I'm not sure yet."

My history class was filled with interesting people who had significant life experiences that fascinated me. Many of them were "older" students who had returned to college to finally earn their degree. My self-confidence grew as my history professor welcomed my visits to his office, answered my questions about wrong answers on a test, and suggested ways to expand my topic for a research paper.

In my English courses, teachers recognized the way I listened to them. I internalized their ideas and added my own. In my major courses, I wasn't made to feel like I didn't know what I was doing, or that my thoughts didn't matter.

That's not what I remember about the big university in Austin, and taking classes with my boyfriend. The classes were so big that no professor knew my name. If my boyfriend was in the class, he monopolized my time, and we spent time outside of classes with his ROTC friends and no one else.

Who was this person, Diane Theresa Gonzales? When my Texas history professor asked me to take the next class he was teaching, I enrolled, even though history wasn't my major. By the end of the spring semester, I became a double major and loved every minute of my courses in English and history.

By then I knew I wanted to be a teacher. I started to take an active role in my education and enrolled in courses that interested me. Unfortunately, my courses didn't fit into my boyfriend's schedule. We took our own cars to the university the following year. Sometimes we saw each other at lunch. He was working for my father by then, so we saw each other after work or school.

Coming back to San Antonio also set into motion other events that would change my love life, too. The fall semester of my senior year, I met an old friend at church and continued to see him every Sunday. Eventually, I ended my relationship with my old boyfriend and started dating the man I would eventually marry.

I imagine that some people think that going away to college, only to return two years later, could be a failure of sorts. However, returning to my hometown, to a brand-new university where the students were anxious to learn, not party, gave me a chance to discover who I was.

As I remember this time of my life, I see that my identity had formed as an individual. I became a person separate from my parents, my family, and my boyfriend. I realize now that a person doesn't have to leave home for college to "separate" and become an individual. We become individuals when we make the time to discover our own true name, and learn to say it proudly.

DIANE GONZALES BERTRAND

THE REAL WINNER

I *was so excited. My brother, Neal, and I told our parents* goodbye and off we went to my dress rehearsal. I had been selected as a contestant for the upcoming Miss Teenage Pageant. I had asked Neal to go along with me.

"Sure. The benefits will be out of this world," he laughingly replied. The week before the dress rehearsal he dreamed of the thirty-seven other girls who would be walking across the stage. He gladly accompanied me, but only to keep me from being alone, of course.

For months before the big day, I practiced my gymnastic routine on my front lawn. With my stereo blasting out the window, I turned somersaults and cartwheels. I taught myself to turn flips in midair and also learned to do backbends with ease. As the music played, I tumbled. The neighbors were tired of hearing the same song over and over, day after day, but they knew that this skinny fourteen-year-old girl had a dream to compete, so they kept quiet.

"It's almost time, Neal," I whispered, during dress rehearsal that Sunday afternoon.

"Go show them who's the best," Neal said, as he smiled.

I took my stance on stage and the very familiar song began to play. I felt so elegant, so graceful, and for the first time in my life I felt like somebody special. I never expected to win. I realized that I couldn't compete with the shapely seniors, but I had worked very hard to secure a place in the lineup just the same.

About midway through my routine, I took an awkward flip and landed with both big toes bent down. Intense pain hit both feet at the same time. Regardless, I continued with my routine. Neal sensed the pain in my face. As I ran offstage to the dressing room, he followed me and waited outside. I cried as I walked out and showed him my feet and legs. They were black and blue from the tips of my toes to above both knees. I knew immediately that I had either sprained or broken both of my big toes.

The first night of the pageant was scheduled for the next evening. Both Neal and I shuddered to think that my dream had been broken, along with the bones in my toes. We spoke very few words as we drove home to break the news to my parents. I thought about the amount of money they had spent on my different outfits—especially the formal gown. Once we arrived home, my parents knew immediately that something was wrong when they saw Neal helping me out of the car. When I showed them my feet and legs, Daddy said, "You know you can't tumble tomorrow night, don't you, honey?"

"Yes I can," I said, as tears filled my eyes.

"I have a great idea," my mother exclaimed, trying to find a better way. "You can play the piano." I sat down to play my rendition of the last piece I played in a piano recital, when I was seven years old. Somehow, "Twelve Gray Dwarfs" wasn't as impressive when I played it as a teenager.

I heard my family snicker. When I looked around, everyone hushed and tried to refrain from laughing. We all decided that the only real talent that I had was gymnastics. If I couldn't turn cartwheels and flips, I could forget competing in the pageant.

The next afternoon, Daddy wrapped tape tightly around my toes. I practiced walking in my high heel shoes. Walking elegantly in my formal dress shoes was very painful, but my determination was strong. Just before the time came to leave, Daddy hugged me.

"Are you sure you want to do this, honey?" he asked. "You know you don't have to."

"I'm sure," I said, as I limped out to the car.

When we arrived at the Grand Opera House for the two-night

event, I pasted on a smile and tried to pretend that I wasn't in pain. When it came my turn for the talent competition, I took my stance for the first time since the accident. Even though hundreds of people were present, you could have heard a pin drop once the music began. I saw the stage curtains open. On the first beat, I began my performance. It was a perfect show—probably the best I had ever done. As the music came to a close, the emcee announced that I performed my gymnastics routine with two broken toes. I received a standing ovation and went home with my head held high.

Before the twelve finalists were picked the following night, all of the contestants were lined up backstage. Our hearts were pounding. I heard the back door open, just before we were to walk out onstage to find out who would be the one to wear the crown home. One of the pageant officials called my name. "Would you please come back here for a second?" she asked.

After approaching the back door, a lady whom I had never seen before hugged me. "My eight-year-old son couldn't be here tonight," she said. "He was sick. He made me promise to tell you that you are his favorite contestant. He also wanted you to know that even if you don't win the crown, you are still the real winner."

My heart was touched. I felt like the most beautiful girl onstage. I wasn't sure how many people I had impressed with my performance the night before, but I knew I had impressed one little guy for sure.

Soon the twelve finalists were named. The girls chosen jumped up and down, screaming at the top of their lungs. I stood quietly with the remaining girls in line. While some of them were crying, I wasn't that disappointed, because I didn't expect to win in the first place. Before the night was over, one of the shapely seniors was announced as the winner, just as I had expected.

I didn't wear the crown home that night, but I didn't quit either. I felt proud that a boy I didn't even know thought I was the real winner. For what more can a winner ask than for someone to believe in her and have the desire for her to win? I went home with a smile on my face and a joyful feeling in my heart.

Today, when I watch beauty pageants on television, my heart flutters when the winner's is called. But then I think of the little boy and wonder if the real winner was the one who actually wore the crown home. The real winner of the contest just might have been the skinny contestant who did her best regardless of the difficulties set before her.

NANCY B. GIBBS

BARNYARD TAE KWON DO

I've *been involved in Tae Kwon Do for six years. In ad-*
dition to teaching the techniques, forms, and discipline
involved, my instructor also has taught me about Aims of
Achievement. These include things like perseverance, courtesy,
integrity, and self-control. They apply not only to martial arts, but
to everyday life as well, even on the farm!

Kids in my school are seriously into animals. Living in the
country, everyone knows you sleep with your boots on and spend
your time pampering pigs, sheep, and cows. Most of the nearly
three hundred students in my combined middle and high school
are involved in livestock shows in one way or another.

Not wanting to be left out, I pleaded with my folks for animals
of my own. At first, they hemmed and hawed over the time it
would take. My father is a veterinarian, and he knows what it
takes to care for animals. Since I was already committed to Tae
Kwon Do, they worried I'd flake out before receiving my black
belt. They should have known that wasn't an option. Hanging in
there, no matter what, is one of the important lessons my martial
arts teacher taught me.

Contrary to what you might believe, sheep are not cuddly, cute,
or white. My first lamb was seventy pounds of three-inch-thick
wool, brown from mud, and he had black heels that always
wound up in my face. He directed all of his pent-up energy into
knocking me down to get to the feed. I even got knocked out cold
one time by the pushy lamb—something that never happened to
me in Tae Kwon Do. After two months of my convincing him that

I wasn't going to eat him each time I went into his pen, he finally settled down and looked forward to feeding time.

Then I wound up with a pig that had a mind of his own, and a calf that had nearly no mind at all. Juggling schoolwork, the animals, and Tae Kwon Do had me running every minute. Yet, after pestering my folks, I wasn't about to give up on any of it.

Not losing my cool became yet another barnyard application of Tae Kwon Do. In the wee hours on cold, rainy mornings, I had to force myself out of my nice warm bed and go feed my sheep. Sometimes the little critter would break out of its pen, happy to be free. No amount of pleading, crying, or chasing convinced my prancing bundle of joy to come back. I finally discovered that placing a bowl of feed where I wanted him to be accomplished much more. Sometimes the quiet approach worked far better than my frantic efforts—another barnyard lesson in Tae Kwon Do.

By the time I began inching my way toward my brown belt, I'd started showing my sheep. I learned that courtesy was essential to a successful showing. I received instructions on how to hold my sheep close to me, how to feed and groom him, and how to show respect and shake the judge's hand in thanks—even when I didn't place well. There is no way to go to a sheep show with about four hundred animals present and not help each other out. In my last show, I watched a ten-year-old child copy my every move and learn from me. Again, I am reminded of Tae Kwon Do.

At last, the time came for me to train for my black belt. What better time to take on a new herd of lambs? Four of them.

At a winter livestock show the judge commented that I'd shown a different sheep in every event. He asked how many I had. When I told him he said, "Tough as nails in the spirit department." *The sheep, or me?* I wondered, thinking again of martial arts.

That night, I brought my sheep home from showing them. They were shaved for the show, and everything from their eyes to their shivering bodies said, "Brrrrr!" I hated to see them so cold, so I spent five hours sewing green sheep blankets. They looked like horse blankets, only on a smaller scale. I hung in there making sure the lambs were covered. I noticed the next morning that they showed their appreciation by eating the blankets!

Through thick and thin and the practice of Tae Kwon Do, my sheep and I have persevered. I'm not sure that I would have been as successful in one without the other. I do know I'm a different person than I would have been without being challenged to apply what I'd learned in class in my own backyard. My parents are proud of me because it now seems clear that I earned my "black belt" in the barnyard long before achieving it on the mat practicing Tae Kwon Do.

ALANA JENKINS

I had never stolen before. It was Gail's thirteenth birthday and Gail, Chris, and I had decided to go downtown to the five-and-dime to browse the candy section. While they made their decision between Almond Joy and Nestle Crunch, I spotted the box of Mr. Goodbars, picked one up, and slipped it into my jacket pocket. My friends didn't even notice. As we made our way into the line and waited our turn, we talked about what we were going to do next. Listening to Chris, I felt smug about that candy bar and about how sly I was to have slipped it in my pocket.

The cashier rang up Chris's and then Gail's candy bars. Just a few more seconds, and we would be out of the store. Then I could show my friends exactly how cool I was. The cashier collected the money and put the candy bars in a small bag. Chris picked up the bag and made her way to the end of the cashier's counter with Gail behind her. Just as I was about to follow, I heard a woman's voice.

"Would you like to pay for what's in your pocket?"

I raised my head to find the cashier looking directly at me. I could feel my heart suddenly pounding in my chest.

"Are you going to pay for the candy in your pocket?"

I froze in the beam of her stare. I thought no one had seen. I slowly reached into my pocket, pulled out the candy, and placed it on the counter. Chris and Gail stared at me, not quite sure what was going on. The clerk rang it up—I think it totaled all of twenty-five cents—and I paid for it before the manager escorted me to the back of the store. My friends were instructed to wait outside.

The manager took me to her office and told me to sit down on the straight-backed chair by the door. She fixed me with a stare and said, "Shoplifting is a crime." I began to tremble and felt tears well up in my eyes.

"Are you going to call the police?" I asked, my voice quavering.

"No," replied the manager. "But I am going to call your parents, and you're going to tell them what happened. I want you to write down your telephone number and then wait right here while I call."

I wrote down my phone number and with a shaky hand gave her the paper. She took it and began to dial. A hot tear slid down my cheek. I brushed at it, but another one followed. I was far from being cool now. Watching the manager dial the number was torture. I waited for the inevitable. And waited. And waited.

"It seems that no one's home," she said.

I took a deep breath. *I am saved,* I thought. *My mom won't find out about this, and I can just pretend it never happened.*

"I want you to write down your name and your parents' names on this paper," the manager said, interrupting my relief.

"Why?"

"Because when you get home, you need to have one of your parents call me and let me know that you told them what happened. Here's my business card. If I don't receive a call from your mom or dad today, I'll call the police. Do you understand?"

I nodded my head and put the business card into my pants pocket. After a few more minutes, she walked me back to the front of the store. To my relief, Chris and Gail had waited for me.

On the walk home they pumped me for information. Reluctantly, I told them about the straight-backed chair by the door and the unanswered call home, showed them the manager's business card, and told them about the proposed call to the police if I didn't follow through and tell my parents. Repeating it all made my stomach lurch.

"Why did you do it?" Chris asked.

"I don't know," I said. "To be cool, I guess." I really had no good reason and hadn't stopped ahead of time to think of the consequences. I'd had an itch and I'd scratched it. Now the angry welt of reality was rising.

The walk home was torture. For twenty minutes I agonized over how I was going to tell Mom that she didn't have a perfect little Miss Goodbar after all. I felt ashamed, and scared that somehow she wouldn't love me the same. Chris and Gail had listened as my tale unraveled and made sympathetic noises, which helped, until my driveway came into view. From there on, it was clear I was on my own.

I stood at the foot of my driveway, watching as they neared the corner and as a last toehold on something solid called out, "Happy Birthday, Gail." Before Gail's name had traveled the space between us, they disappeared.

My mother's car was parked in front of the house. After a deep breath, I hiked up the steep driveway. She was in the living room reading a magazine. I slid the now damp business card from my pocket and pressed it between my palms as I sat on the footstool in front of her. The well-worn upholstery of the stool sank under my weight. Mom's brows pulled together as I spilled my story. Her lips leveled off in a tight line as her disappointment washed over me. After I finished, she wordlessly rose and phoned the store manager to confirm that I'd told her what I'd done.

When she got off the phone, she said, "You're grounded. For a month." Had I been standing, my legs would have buckled under the weight of her disapproval and, in spite of my friends' company and support, the isolation and embarrassment I'd felt on the walk home. To this day there's not a Mr. Goodbar I see or a candy aisle I pass without a flinch of remorse. I ask you, how cool is that?

ROBIN MICHELLE MENDOZA

IV
BRINGING SPIRIT
TO LIFE

Put your ear down close to your soul and listen hard.

ANNE SEXTON

Sometimes people come into our lives
for a reason, a season, or a lifetime.
AUTHOR UNKNOWN

OLIVER BASCOM

*I*t is a mystery how I grew to be such a tall girl, but I learned at an early age to cope with my size by trying to be as unremarkable as possible. At school, I wore drab colors and low-heel shoes. I always chose a seat in the back of the room and never raised my hand in class, and with my head down and shoulders stooped, I virtually slouched my way through junior high school.

When I was sixteen, we moved to a small town. I was relatively happy in my new school although still very self-conscious about my height. Whenever we would go to the bleachers for club or class photos, I always wore flat shoes and stood in the back row so I could bend my knees without being seen.

Our teachers were caring and conscientious, and I especially liked my English teacher because she loved to discuss Greek mythology, and she always cried when she read poetry to us. The first day of classes my senior year, however, the school was abuzz with the news that she had left to get married and that we were going to have a new English teacher, Oliver Bascom.

Oliver Bascom! He had to be a close relative of Mr. Peepers with a name like that! My girlfriends and I doubled over with laughter as we conjured up visions of a short, bald, skinny, prune-faced Caspar Milquetoast wearing horn-rimmed glasses and plaid pants. The situation wasn't really funny, because we were going to have to endure this man for the entire year. As we lethargically made our way to class, we were determined to find seats as far back in the room as possible.

We arrived just before the tardy bell, opened the door, and there, in front of the blackboard, descended directly from Mount Olympus and on loan to us for the whole year, stood Adonis. He was tall and young and handsome and had the classic chiseled features of a Greek statue and a body that inspired many a dream that night.

What ensued was sheer pandemonium, a melee of seventeen-year-old girls, flying elbows and feet, scrambling to get to seats in the front of the room. With my long legs and arms, I managed to secure the front-row-center desk. The boys ended up in the back of the room where they virtually disappeared for the rest of the year.

I was desperate to make a good impression on my new teacher but kept quiet because I didn't have anything interesting to say. The day that directions were given for our first major writing assignment, I arrived late to class. A friend later gave me the guidelines and I thought I understood them. I worked the entire weekend on the essay, turned it in on time, and waited anxiously for Mr. Bascom's evaluation.

After three or four days, he arrived in class bearing a stack of the corrected papers, which he put on the desk in two piles.

"I've selected the ten best essays for class comment and discussion," he said.

Twenty minutes later, my heart sank when he got to the last composition in the pile, and I realized that mine had not made the top ten. Oh, where to hide? Why had I ever chosen the most exposed desk in the room?

"These are all outstanding efforts," Mr. Bascom continued

"however, I am now going to read you the most successful of all, a composition that is completely different from the rest and that is remarkable for its originality and creativity." He pulled a paper out of his briefcase and began to read. We all dropped our jaws as it dawned on us that I was the author of this unusual work.

I never told anyone that the reason my composition was so different was because I had totally misunderstood the assignment. Nevertheless, a different girl walked out of the classroom that day. I knew that I had a new set of standards to live up to and that anything was possible in the future. On my way to my next class, I could actually feel my spine stretch as I raised my head and straightened my shoulders.

Oliver Bascom was an incomparable teacher and under his guidance we learned to write well and to appreciate good literature. During that year we read Plato, T. S. Eliot, Dylan Thomas, Tennessee Williams, and Chaucer in the original Middle English. After studying *Hamlet,* he took the class to San Francisco to see the play. I was inconsolable when I got the flu and had to stay home.

A week later, with permission from my parents and his wife, Mr. Bascom took me, all by myself, to the city for dinner and to see the play. As we left the restaurant, he gallantly offered his arm to escort me down Geary Boulevard toward the playhouse. I was glad that I was wearing a bright orange dress and had exchanged my flat loafers for three-inch spike heels, because for the first time that I could remember, I wanted the whole world to see me.

KATHLEEN PIMENTEL

GETTIN' MY MOJO WORKIN'

ack when I was no bigger than a tadpole, I enjoyed **B** lounging with my buddies on the pink chenille bed-spread of Stella Roberts, who had her own apartment behind the big house of the Dean Pearman family in our quiet little Mississippi Delta town. This was a black-white situation, you see, back in the early fifties. Stella was the maid, and we little white neighborhood girls were her loyal subjects. We adored her, and she ruled the roost in this little racially segregated corner of the universe.

Ahhh, did she ever rule. Kathy, Judy, and I sprawled on Stella's bed, stringing beads and eating crackers, listening to blues and barrelhouse music on the radio, while Stella danced around the tiny, bare room, throwing her head back, waving her arms, moving her hips. We'd watch and question her.

"Stella, how come you don't like Perry Como? Or Dinah Shore? How come you like music like that?"

She'd laugh big and say, "Girls, one day you'll find out what real music is. One day you'll find out what moves your soul."

The next thing we knew our mamas were saying to us, "Y'all can't go hang out at Stella's anymore on Saturday afternoons. You don't need to be listening to that trashy music." Then we gave Judy a heap of hassle because she told her daddy about some of the words—mighty mild lyrics compared with what's out there today, for sure. Anyway, at that point we didn't know a thing about being lovesick or having powerful ways. Fact is we weren't too knowledgeable about much of anything.

Well, we did know a couple of things. We knew Stella could sure get down with the dancing, and we knew we girls were happy as little pine borers in a fresh log. The really big thing we didn't realize as we hung out with Stella and her wonderful music was that we were hearing the birth, right then, of rock and roll. Two years later, Mississippi-born Elvis Presley combined rhythm-and-blues and gospel, and there you have it.

Stella wasn't around the neighborhood two years later, though. She went off and left us. Headed up Highway 61 with her one little bag of possessions, moving to Chicago, hoping to find a better life. But as Kathy, Judy, and I entered our teenage years, we never forgot her. Thanks to Stella, we three took a back seat to none on the dance floor. We were the sock hop queens because of our training on the polished hardwood of Stella's tiny one-room quarters. She was the best. She put our mojos in high gear early on and taught us, yes indeed, what truly moves a young girl's soul.

BETH BOSWELL JACKS

While watching a movie the other night, I was very moved by a scene in which a small boy, obviously on his way to school, is following a group of his classmates down a back alley. The boy is calling in a frantic voice to his friends, "Wait up, wait up!" He stumbles along half running, half walking, trying to catch up with them. Instead of waiting for him, they are tossing back insults and jeers, calling him a baby and ordering him to leave them alone. One glance at the small boy tells you that he does not fit in.

When I was thirteen years old, my father accepted a position teaching at a university in another province, and we moved during the summer. The first day of the tenth grade found me sitting beside my mother in the car outside the front of the school, wishing I were dead. Groups of kids stood around laughing and talking. I knew that any minute, my mother was going to expect me to exit the car and face the judge, jury, and executioner, also known as my peer group. No Christian felt any less terror facing the lions than I felt that morning.

An accelerated elementary school program had put me in the less-than-enviable position of being thirteen years old going into the tenth grade. Not only was I younger in chronological years, I was physically small and emotionally younger as well. Mercifully, the sound of a loud buzzer sent the groups of kids into the school. At least now I wouldn't have to walk past hundreds of appraising and critical eyes. My mother put her hand on my arm. "You had better get going so you won't be late."

I wondered how she could be so casual about my doom. I decided if she loved me, she wouldn't make me do this. My fear of facing the day was now matched by my anger at her for not understanding and alleviating my agony.

Somehow I made it into the school and found my homeroom and assigned desk. A quick glance around me confirmed my worst suspicions. Every single thing about me was wrong. I looked at the girls sitting nearby. I saw long, thick hair, makeup expertly applied, stylish clothes, and breasts. They all had breasts. In contrast, I sat there with my short, childish haircut, my face devoid of makeup and framed by thick black glasses, my infantile clothes, and the body of a ten-year-old boy. I begged God to open up the earth at that precise moment and swallow me. How in heaven's name was I going to make it through homeroom, much less through the entire year? Like the small boy in the movie, I waited for my peers to turn on me. I had been through it many times, and I knew how it worked. The glances, the whispers, and finally the silence would all tell me that I did not belong and never would.

Suddenly a voice behind me said, "You're new here, aren't you?"

I sighed and turned around. *Here it goes,* I thought. I made eye contact with an extremely pretty girl, and I realized with a shock that the look on her face was kind and that she was smiling.

"I was new last year," she said, "and I know how hard it can be. My name is Sue Breffit."

Her beautiful brown eyes sparkled, and her voice was reassuring.

"You'll be just fine."

I was too stunned to reply, and the teacher's voice commanding our attention prevented any further communication.

We did not speak again that morning, but over the next year Sue would often appear out of nowhere to say hello and ask me how things were going. She was one of the most popular girls in

school, and I could never understand why she took the time to as-
sociate with a misfit like me. Perhaps I should have asked her. I
never got the chance, because she was killed in a car accident during the summer before grade eleven. When her death was announced at the start of school that fall, I grieved for my guardian
angel.

Years later, I was reading the newspaper and I saw a memo-
rial notice under the name "Breffit." Reading the notice I was
surprised to realize that Sue had been dead for twelve years.
Her mother's name appeared at the bottom, and for a moment I
longed to tell Mrs. Breffit about her daughter. I'm sure she knew
that Sue had been good-looking, clever, and popular. What she
didn't know was that her daughter had rescued a drowning girl
the first terrible day of school.

Susan B. Townsend

Destiny doesn't exist. It's God we need, and fast.
ADÉLIA PRADO

SEEK AND YOU SHALL FIND

*I*n my early twenties, I completed an undergrad program in the Midwest to become a social worker. Immediately afterward, I made a bold move and relocated to
Florida to work with troubled youth in a very impoverished area.
One night, I attended a meeting, with a coworker, for the Big
Brother/Big Sister program in an old building smack dab in the
middle of a crime-ridden neighborhood.

The meeting went late, and my coworker left me with instructions to lock up. I escorted all of the volunteers out, said my good-
byes, shut off the lights, locked the building, and handed the keys
to one of the volunteers.

I crossed the parking lot and watched everyone drive away.
When I walked up to my old Chevy hatchback, I saw my car keys
on the front seat! Panic set in as I realized that the doors were
locked to my car, the building was locked, and everyone was
gone. Being a fairly resourceful person, I quickly summed up my
options. I could either wait with my car until someone came by,
which might not be until morning, or walk in the hope of finding
a phone or someone to help me.

I had not worked in the city long, but I knew that there were
several drug houses nearby and a long history of shootings and

other violence surrounding this neighborhood. I specifically re-called a coworker telling me, "Always go into this part of town in the morning with someone else." Well, here I was at 11 P.M., all alone, feeling frightened and vulnerable. My anxiety grew as I crossed a very dark stretch of grass. There were no streetlights and only the sound of cars in the distance, yelling, music, sirens, and perhaps my own loud heartbeat.

The only thing I could think to do was to pray. I did not know where I was headed, whom I would meet up with, or what would happen. With each step, I crushed empty cans, old bottles, and a wealth of other discarded trash. I began walking faster and faster and became frustrated because I had caught something on my foot that I could not shake off. Violently shaking my foot, I ur-gently prayed some more, "Please, God, help me out of this." I suddenly sensed that I was not alone.

Walking several more yards, I couldn't stand it any longer and bent down to remove the irritant. There, on my shoe, was a wire clothes hanger, wrapped so closely around my foot, I had to pull it off. Within seconds, I realized that what I was given wasn't the parting of the Red Sea, but a solution.

I ran back to my car, popped open the lock using the hanger, and sat down in the front seat. Feeling great relief, I held the car keys in my hand and began to cry. What a wonderful life it is when you get a chance to see the One who has all the answers help you to find yours.

KIM KEENAN

REMEMBERING JESS

*E*ven though *Jessica and I had just completed our* sophomore year, we had already planned out our next two years. It was going to be great. By our senior year, we would rule the school! But just a month before our junior year at Cloverleaf Senior High School, everything changed.

I remember receiving the news as if it were yesterday. I was coming home on a school bus with the boys' soccer team after they had finished a preseason game. I saw my sister's car trailing behind us and wondered what she was doing.

She ran up to me the moment I stepped off the bus.

"I have some very bad news," she said. "Jessica was killed in a car accident."

I just stared at her.

"And Jenny is in the hospital in serious condition," she added.

How could this be? I thought. *I just saw them!*

I knew that Jenny was driving Jessica to a volleyball picnic. Apparently, she ran a stop sign and didn't see the supply truck until it was too late. The truck plowed into Jesse's side.

My mind raced. *If I had asked Jess to go to the soccer game with me, this would have never happened!*

I couldn't sleep that night. I tried to think of everything Jess and I had done together because I never wanted to forget her. I went through our whole friendship, angry and annoyed when things didn't come clearly. *Some friend I turned out to be,* I thought.

Exhausted after a sleepless night, I wrapped myself in a blanket and sat on the back deck watching the sunrise. I listened to the gentle singing of the birds when a hummingbird flew in and hovered there just an arm's length away. I didn't reach out to touch the bird for fear of scaring it. Instead, I just watched in silence.

At Jessica's wake, I told her mom about my unusual experience. She told me that it wasn't surprising at all. Hummingbirds were Jesse's favorite creatures!

While sharing stories with her mom, I learned that Jess always said I was too hard on myself. She thought that I shouldn't take things so seriously, and I should try to have some fun every now and then. That was a hard concept to grasp, since I always tried to have everything be perfect.

Ever since I was small, I wanted to be the best. I had to get A's on everything. I wanted to graduate with honors. I played soccer, took band, sang in show choir, and held leadership positions in the honor society and student council. I wanted to show everyone that I could be the ideal student and handle with ease all the responsibilities given to me.

But I was doing too much. I became anxious and nervous all the time. It got to the point where it was hard for me to get out of bed in the mornings because I was still tired from the day before.

Losing Jesse has taught me a lot. Slowly, I am learning life is way too short to be worrying about things over which I have no control. A's aren't everything. Passing up a leadership role doesn't mean I can't be involved. And it's okay to let someone else be the star athlete or best singer. My stepping back means someone else has the opportunity to shine. Now I can appreciate the things in life I miss when I'm too busy to notice. Like the way my brothers and sisters joke, sunrise on a warm summer's day, giggles with a friend, but most of all, sitting on the back deck surrounded by birdsong, waiting for the glimpse of a hummingbird.

Five years have passed since Jesse's death, and I am a senior in college. Now and then I begin to worry and feel uncertain about my future when I finish school. But then I stop and remember that everything will work out if I focus instead on the things that I hold most dear. To help remind me is a Helen Keller quote engraved on Jessica's tombstone. It reads, "The best and most beautiful things in the world cannot be seen or even touched. They must be felt with the heart."

BETH ZIEMNIK

Learning, learning,
and eventually,
learning to forgive others
comes sweetly,
like the fresh-air healing
of a clean-bright ocean breeze,
now inside of me

but to forgive my-
self, to forgive
myself for giving
power to the stones
of my fears; for
controlling others
as if I had to;
for competing and
separating; for not
speaking authentically;
for giving up in big
and little ways; and
for not allowing Love
to sweep through me,
and give me life again—

to forgive myself,
how do I do that?

And Spirit answered
simply, as if looking down
upon a pool of sorrows and regrets

Throw rose petals on it . . .
I heard within my heart!

Then what?
Then love it.
Love it until it changes.
Until in your very Self it changes—
       into the flower of a learning.
       into the sky of a generous teaching.
       into the breath of a blessing
       so great—

You ask it to Stay.

SHEILA STEPHENS

FRIENDS FOREVER

Molly and I were best friends in high school, and what made our friendship so much fun was that we could be goofy together. I cracked her up singing Muppet-version Christmas carols in Miss Piggy's voice and got her to sing along. We had contests to see which one of us could stuff the most grapes into her mouth. At the first hint of snow, we began messy snowball fights that ended in breathless laughter, drowned-rat hair, and a serious need for hot cocoa.

One of our favorite pastimes was visiting our secret crushes—*secret* being the key word. Our crushes were oblivious to our affections, but that didn't stop us from hoping for the near-impossible. Fortunately for us, the two guys lived only a few houses apart. This meant frequent Friday-night drives with the two of us cruising repeatedly up and down the same cul-de-sac, trying to look oh-so-casual in Mom's Volvo. We prayed for a glimpse of our guys, giggling uncontrollably and ducking down whenever a curious resident would peer from behind living-room curtains, probably wondering why any car would have cause to circle the block for twenty minutes straight. We swore that someday we'd actually ring the guys' doorbells.

Unrequited love can make you hungry, so we went out to eat often. One day we were sitting at a booth in a restaurant, enjoying lunch, when I made a joke. Unfortunately for Molly, she found it funny. Her laughter sounded something like this: "Ha-ha-ha, ha-ha-ha—GAAAACK!"

It was the sound of a french fry being inhaled. Molly's eyes widened, her eyebrows rose, and her lips parted in shock. Now, choking is never funny—except when it's Molly. The look on her face was priceless, as if it genuinely surprised her that she couldn't breathe fries. I burst into laughter. I also managed to ask if she was okay, and after a brief coughing fit, her coughing turned into laughter as loud as my own.

Lunch continued, and soon I jokingly appointed myself as a member of the "fashion police" and began critiquing the outfits on people passing by. Molly was a great audience, giggling at my quips, so I quickly scanned the place for another fashion victim.

"You think that girl had bad taste?" I said. "Check that out." I pointed out the window toward the front of the restaurant. The car that had just pulled up was coated in a sickly chartreuse color; it looked like one giant late-stage bruise.

"Why would you actually spend money to buy a car that ugly?" I continued. Molly turned around to look out the window then looked back at me.

"That's my mom's car," she said. "She's here to pick us up."

I was horrified. The look on my face was obviously priceless; Molly dissolved into laughter. We walked outside, and I saw that the car wasn't an ugly shade of yellow-green at all; it was actually a pale gray that had absorbed the reflection of the restaurant's splashy neon sign. I spent the next ten minutes apologizing and trying to explain myself while Molly and her mom laughed.

Graduation day came quickly. Molly was a year younger, so she would be staying behind at school as I went off to college across the country. We were both heartbroken that we wouldn't be near enough to spend time together anymore, but we vowed to stay close at heart. She signed my yearbook "Best friends forever!"

I saw Molly only a few times during the next couple of years. Nearly all of my other close friends were college students like me, and we had long conversations about our new lives. We talked about classes, internships, and potential careers. We talked about dorm food, cute resident advisers, and wild parties. We loved having no parents to report to, but we were discovering the downside of independence too; suddenly we had to do our own laundry, pay our own bills, and kill our own bugs—even the really big ones.

Meanwhile, Molly was still in the town I'd left behind, living at home. She finished high school and took a job at a grocery store. Our lives progressed in different directions, and without our sharing common experiences, the letters and calls eventually stopped. It wasn't that I didn't care for her anymore, but I didn't know what to say. We'd grown apart.

Ten years after high school graduation, my longtime friend Lori ran into Molly. Molly told Lori she'd love to hear from me, so Lori gave me Molly's phone number. At home, I stared at the slip of paper nervously. Should I call? After all this time?

I picked up the phone and dialed.

Talking to Molly was like going back in time to relive the best parts of high school. We laughed about the past and shared what we'd done in the last decade. I felt instantly comfortable, and soon we started hanging out again.

Being with Molly still has the tendency to make me break out in giggles. She laughs easily—even at herself—and after all these years, I still see in her the person I remember from high school, a kindhearted friend whose smiles are frequent and genuine.

Today our lifestyles and our hopes for the future are as different as ever, but now I realize those differences never had to cause us to grow apart. While I'll always need friends who can relate to what's meaningful to me at the time—be that college, career, or marriage—there will always be room in my life for people like Molly. Besides, our friendship never depended as much on what our adventures were as much as it depended on how we approached them. We would end our outings with stomach muscles sore from laughing, and when things went wrong, Molly's easygoing, often-goofy attitude would remind me it's okay to not take life too seriously. We don't need to understand every choice the other has made as long as we can find something to laugh about together.

I don't know whether Molly and I will always stay in touch, but I do know we can be "friends forever" in spirit, because the need for laughter in my life is something I'll never outgrow.

ALAINA SMITH

V
TEEN MISCHIEF

I can sometimes resist temptation, but never mischief.

JOYCE REBETA-BURDITT

SOMETIMES YOU JUST CAN'T WIN

*M*y grandparents raised me. When I was fourteen years old, my grandmother died unexpectedly, so in an instant, I became the lady of the house. At fifteen, I received my hardship driver's license. The year was 1970 and disco was all the rage. Oh, how I loved to trip the lights fantastic!

Sometimes at night, after my grandfather was fast asleep, I'd sneak out, "borrow" the car, and go dancing at the local discotheque. The trick was to return the car and get back into bed before his alarm went off at 4:30 A.M.

The first thing he did when he got up every morning was to come straight into my room and "eyeball" me, making sure I was fast asleep in my bed where I belonged.

One night while returning home, I executed my usual clever routine, which began by turning off the headlights three or four houses down from mine and coasting into the driveway. Next, I tiptoed up the steps and entered the house, but just as I was about to close the door, I heard a loud crash. *Yikes!* The car was sitting across the street in the neighbor's yard! I had forgotten to put it in park, so the car had rolled out of the driveway, across the street, over a curb, and into a tree.

I quickly retrieved the car, put it in park this time, and hurried into the house. I hopped into bed and was pulling the covers over my clothes just as my grandfather entered my room. *Whew!*

What a narrow escape. Or was it? After he got to work the next morning and noticed the dent in the rear bumper of the car, he called me.

"Sherry Lynne, what the devil happened to the car?"

At first, I squirmed and played innocent, but finally I confessed. When we met up at home that evening, the first thing he did was to test my story by putting the car in reverse and floorboarding it out of the driveway. But no matter how many times he did this (and believe me, he did it a lot!), the car would *not* jump the curb and hit that tree. He became obsessed. He wouldn't come in for dinner, and I'm not sure he ever went to bed because I was hiding in my room, afraid to come out. What had I done? I had turned my granddaddy into a raving maniac!

Over the next twenty years of my life, I can't tell you how many times he repeated this exercise unsuccessfully. It always resulted in the same old appeal, "Sherry Lynne, just tell me the truth about what happened to the car."

I gave the same old reply. "Granddaddy, I *did* tell you the truth. That's what really happened."

Very near the end of his life, I went to visit him in the hospital. When he saw me coming through the door, he beckoned me with his index finger to come in close. He was very frail and could hardly speak, but still, I heard that familiar plea, "Sherry Lynne, just tell me the truth about what happened to the car."

This time though, I broke down. "Granddaddy, *please,* I can't stand you thinking that I've been lying to you for all these years. That really *is* what happened."

He winked and said, "Come here, baby." As he held me in his arms for one of the last times, he whispered, "Sherry Lynne, I know you weren't lying, but I just couldn't let a granddaughter of mine grow up thinking she was clever by sneaking around."

He was right, I had thought I was clever. Worse, I thought he could be fooled because he was old and had no idea of what it was like to be a teenager. He gave me a hug and with a twinkle in his eye said, "You remind me of myself a long time ago. Don't forget, I was young once too."

Sherry Bennett

CONFESSIONS OF
A WEEKEND HIPPIE

I *grew up in New Jersey in the town near the George*
Washington Bridge, which connects New Jersey to Manhattan. We weren't allowed to go into Manhattan without
our parents. We were very sheltered. According to our moms,
there was no "reason" to go into New York.

At the time, we broke a lot of rules.

We could never see the whole picture our parents saw, such as
the potential dangers or our naïveté. We had just heard about a
peace rally and our antennae went up. Peace rallies were for college kids, and seemed like a great way to meet some of them. And
they were a way to meet guys.

I was smart enough to know how to participate on the outer
fringes of an antiwar conversation if I had to. I even practiced in
the mirror giving the peace sign with my fingers. But the communal, antimaterialistic, live-off-the-fruit-of-the-earth, free-loving,
anti-armpit-shaving, take-a-shower-with-a-friend life was not for
me. All I wanted was a cute boyfriend with long hair.

The only thing hippie about me was my clothes, and even that
was fabricated. I thought I looked so good. You know those pictures they put in textbooks now with hippies wearing Day-Glo
clothes waving peace signs in the sixties? I could have modeled for
those pictures, and I'd have looked more authentic.

I had special glasses with all different colored interchangeable lenses. Some days I looked at the world through pink plastic and some days the world had a blue or lilac hue. I even mixed them to see the world from different perspectives simultaneously.

I had a Jimmy Hendrix floppy-brimmed hat.

I wore my hip-hugger jeans low and tight. To get them on, I had to be flat on my bed. I'd zip them up and then need help to stand up. Sitting wasn't an option. The jeans were bleached in my mother's washing machine and I hand-frayed each leg. It took a lot of work to get them right. I remember my mother huffing about buying expensive jeans for $20 that didn't fit and I was deliberately ruining.

I wore embroidered shirts from India or tie-dyed shirts, which I created, also using and ruining my mother's washing machine.

I had a fringed suede jacket that cost me two months' worth of babysitting money because my parents wouldn't buy it for me. They said I'd leave it somewhere. I did.

I wore sandals in the winter.

And I wore beads. I wore a lot of beads.

The most important part, obviously, was my hair. Since going to peace rallies was planned in advance so we could coordinate our alibis, I had to get my hippie-do just right. It had to look like I did nothing to it. That took hours of twisting, beading, and braiding.

But it was all a façade.

Inside I was a typical teen looking for a place to fit. I've spent a lifetime trying to do the same thing.

My kids think I was a hippie because I am unconventional. I once overheard my son telling someone on the phone, "My mom's not like other moms." I'm not sure if that was meant as a compliment, but it is accurate. I've also heard them tell their friends I used to be a hippie. My cousin showed my kids some pictures of me when I was sixteen, and I guess to them, how I looked back then is proof enough.

I've tried to explain to them that it was all about meeting cute guys with long hair. Then they point to my husband, who has a lot less hair now than he did then, and they laugh.

FELICE R. PRAGER

BIG BUNS

The first time I'd ever shown a pig I was nine years old. I took my duty as a Future Farmer of America seriously and had worked with Big Buns every single day through a summer humid enough to mold barn straw in minutes. I brushed his bristly red hair and taught him to heel and to roll over for tummy scratches.

By the time we arrived at Eufaula, Oklahoma, the day of the show, my mentors Randy and Amanda were sure Big Buns and I were ready. In the show ring, they pointed out all of the gates we'd have to go through and showed me how to approach the judge. Mom kept Big Buns company in his pen. With all those strange pigs and people, the dusty barn was dimmer and more crowded than Big Buns was used to. He paced and blew air through his snout in great forceful grunts, and pawed the straw clear down to the cement floor underneath.

I'd never seen him this riled up and was starting to wonder if I'd be able to get him settled for the show. When his turn at the wash rack came, it took the four of us to herd Big Buns out of the pen and down the aisle. Randy and Amanda stood on each side of him while Mom brought up the rear, and I led the way.

The closer we got to the rack, the more fidgety Big Buns became. He caught a whiff of the soap and heard the squeals of all the other poor pigs being bathed and decided he didn't want any part of it.

With a sudden shove past Amanda, he turned down a side aisle. Amanda leapt in front of him, but ended up under his four flying hooves. She hadn't even slowed him down! Big Buns barreled straight on, heading toward the mother of another Future Farmer. The woman sat in the middle of the aisle in a lawn chair sipping pop beside a big blue cooler. Ray-Bans were propped up in her blonde hair.

As Big Buns got closer I yelled, *"Big Buns, heel!"*

I might as well have saved my breath. With four of us behind him and pens to either side, there was nowhere for him to go but forward, right under the lady's chair. Pop splashed everywhere as the chair lifted and she waved her arms wildly for balance. Big Buns charged forward, not giving a moment's notice to the woman riding him. I don't think she broke eight seconds, but it was quite a ride until she ended up face down in the sawdust.

Mom apologized to the lady who used to be in the lawn chair, while the rest of us ran him down. It took all three of us to half drag and half carry Big Buns to the wash rack.

By the end of the day, he'd gone on to take third in the overall category, but if the judge had seen his skill at bucking riders, he easily would have taken first!

CHERYL JENKINS

Your own sense of style may come in fits and starts,
but trust that it will come, and when it does, it will be glorious.
SARAH BAN BREATHNACH

SHARP EDGES

While I was sanitizing myself in the communal YWCA shower, a woman sloshed in, turned on the faucet, and suctioned her foot to the wall. I tried not to stare as she shaved her leg, but it was hard not to. She maneuvered that razor like an auto racer in the final heat—and not one laceration.

Things go differently for me. A little nick here, a little cut there, and I peer down upon two limbs of "connect the dots." For me to be fashionably correct, it's a blood sacrifice.

Recently poised with razor, styptic pencil, and tourniquet, I was jolted by a memory when shaving was an obsession in my race to maturity.

The reason for my fixation was Sally Zimmer, the femme fatale of my ninth-grade class. She sported cantaloupes while I was training kiwis. Her body rounded in and out; I resembled a sapling. She had luxurious bouncy hair; I had static electricity. But of all her attributes, what did I envy most? Her shaved legs. Smooth and hairless, looking sensational in sheer stockings. My legs in stockings resembled the hairnetted heads of school cafeteria cooks.

The worst humiliation came in swim class. A lukewarm pool at 8 A.M. was insulting enough, but the regulation blue bathing suit added injury to my unripened shape. Then there was Sally—a Pamela Anderson clone. Her legs? Even her thighs were shaved. I examined my own hairy limbs that graced my shapeless body and heard my mother's admonishment: "Don't you dare shave your legs; once you start you can never stop."

My rite of passage came during a Sunday visit to Sally's house. While we studied for an exam, Sally's mother asked her to prepare for a family outing.

"Come on," Sally said, "keep me company while I bathe." I sat on the toilet's lid as Sally filled the tub with bubbled water. She gracefully submerged. Suddenly, a metal instrument materialized in her hand. She glided it deftly up and down her outstretched leg. My eyes rounded like bottle caps, fascinated by such a forbidden ritual.

"Want to try it?" she asked. The razor, suspended in midair, drooled water from hidden chambers, the blade sheltered beneath silver lips. "Yes," I yelped and whipped off my blue jeans.

I remember the exhilaration of seeing the hairs disappear as each swipe mowed a new path. But what was also disappearing was skin. Little red beads crept to the surface. One mingled with another till they surged like angry floodwater. Gashes embroidered my limbs, and before our eyes my skinny legs inflated like puff pastries. The razor I had looked upon with longing and desire had zapped me like an unhinged lover in a betrayal flick.

Sally raced towels and ice into the bathroom and we pressed my oozing legs with all the might of our fourteen years. I was worn down, but she recharged with a stupefying utterance: "You'd better call your mother."

I hobbled with towel-encased legs to the bedroom phone. My index finger dragged over the numbers. "Mom, I can't walk home. Can you get me? Yes . . . a little accident, but I'm fine . . . no . . . when you get here."

I sat on Sally's doorstep and surveyed the damage. My mother pulled her car to the curb—her sharp eyes riveted on my colorful pinstriping. I waited in silence for the predictable lecture, but a miracle happened instead. Her face crinkled and her eyes closed to slits as she collapsed backward in roaring laughter.

"Well," she finally said, "it looks like we'll be shopping for an electric."

Today faded scars accent my legs like thunderbolts of exclamation. And as I dab that blotch of concealer on my newest wound, I'm reminded that Mom was right about shaving—you can never stop—or so I thought.

The other day I bumped into Sally at the mall. She was visiting from California. As we caught up on each other's lives, she told me of the benefits of yoga and macrobiotics. She did have a certain glow, but something else about her appeared different. I subtly scanned her body until my eyes locked on her stockinged legs, which reminded me of the cafeteria cooks.

I thought about Sally throughout the day and decided our chance encounter wasn't by chance at all, but fate's sticky fingers in my unfinished business. I admitted that I'd gotten what I wanted. I willingly traded envy for razor nicks and scars. And as for Sally, maybe deep down all she'd secretly yearned for was a good reason to stop shaving.

SHELLEY SIGMAN

A FAIR TO REMEMBER

I was suspicious from the very start. My teenage daughter and her friend were approaching me with sly smiles and covert looks. Something was certainly up . . . but what? I had spent the better part of the last hour smiling and waving endlessly at my two sweet young sons as they went around yet one more time on the motorcycles at our local county fair. Now I was looking at two older, decidedly more mischievous faces.

"Mom! You just gotta go on this totally awesome ride with us!" exclaimed my fourteen-year-old.

"Yeah!" her best friend eagerly agreed. "We dare you!"

My first instinct was to jump up and down and generally act like a fool because my teenager actually wanted to do something with me. Then the wiser, more experienced voice inside my head took over and reminded me that I was far too old . . . no, not old . . . never old . . . too mature for any of these crazy, wild rides. Those days had been left behind long ago with miniskirts and bell-bottom jeans.

"Which one?" I asked hesitantly, fingers crossed that they somehow meant something tame like the merry-go-round.

"That one!" they exclaimed in unison while grinning at each other.

I looked with mute horror at the ghastly monstrosity they were pointing toward . . . Pharaoh's Fury. It was huge and loud and I could feel the gray hairs popping out of my scalp just thinking about it. There was a line stretching across the county of kids—and only kids—waiting to go on it. Not a person over eighteen was in sight. Surely these girls were jesting. Surely they didn't want this middle-aged mother of four to climb aboard that thing. It defied gravity. It moved faster than the speed of light. It broke the sound barrier.

Ambivalence grabbed hold of me, and I was torn between running away in total cowardice or giving in with dubious acceptance. The ever hopeful mother in me tried to convince myself that here might be a chance to truly bond with my daughter, to perhaps create a lifelong memory, to somehow show her that I was still a hip, cool, groovy mom. The idealistic side gradually won out over the realistic one, and I found myself reluctantly standing in line and paying a surprisingly ridiculous amount of money for this trip into total insanity.

I climbed into the seat, tightly sandwiched between the giggling girls, both looking like the proverbial cats that ate that gullible canary. I had little doubt as to just who the canary was.

The attendant, looking young enough that I knew he had to have been pulled out of elementary school for this job, came by and locked our safety bar. He started to move on but I reached out and grabbed his shoulder and demanded a nonnegotiable "Check it again!" I'm sure I saw him roll his eyes as both girls heaved deep sighs, no doubt feeling quite burdened by this fearful woman and her silly requests. He reached out and pulled on it once more and cast definite "I told you so" looks my way before moving on.

Already I could feel my heartbeat begin to accelerate. My breathing became rapid. My hands were suddenly covered in a cold, clammy sweat. But I was fine, I assured myself; I was okay . . . I was actually doing remarkably well. Of course, it might have been because the ride hadn't started yet.

Now that I was on, I wanted it to start so it'd be over that much faster. To keep myself from vaulting over the safety bar and running back to the comfort of terra firma, I looked at the other fools who were on the ride. Teenager . . . teenager . . . teenager . . . proving once again that they do indeed believe that they are immortal creatures. What? Small children too? How could that be? What parent would put her small child on a death-defying machine like this one? And why were those little faces so much more relaxed than mine was?

I felt the engines rev and the gears begin to shift, and the ride began. For the first one and a half seconds, I was almost normal. This is going to be a piece of cake, I thought. No problem here. I was wrong, incredibly, foolishly wrong. It was even worse than I'd imagined. Within mere seconds, I wasn't smiling, breathing, or screaming. Instead I had plastered myself against the back of the seat, grasping the guardrail for dear life, only letting go long enough to quickly punch my daughter's arm and give her a look that she undoubtedly knew spelled trouble later. How could this confounded contraption ever be considered entertainment? This was torture. Fleetingly, I wondered just when the daredevil teen I used to be had turned into this wimpy mother. Wasn't I the one who once rode roller coasters nonstop in college? When had that daring young girl transformed into this quivering middle-aged woman?

The ride seemed to go on longer than forever. Time slowed down to a snail's pace, just as it does when I'm sitting in the dentist's chair. I desperately tried to distract myself by making out a mental grocery list for the week, but instead found myself frantically writing my will, excluding my daughter completely, of course. I also idly wondered . . . hmm . . . if I threw up, would it go in front of me or behind me?

Finally, blessedly, the ride began to slow down. I felt my pulse begin to slow and my fingers cautiously loosen their death grip on the rail. Already I was beginning to feel calm enough to regret the numerous expletives I'd muttered during the ride, and I hoped my daughter hadn't heard them. As I started to shift sideways to climb out of the car, I felt a hand tap me on the shoulder. An older man in the seat directly behind me gave me a big smile, and I was just sure that he was going to heartily congratulate me on my incredible show of bravery and fortitude.

"Ma'am," he said with a definite Cheshire cat grin, "I saw how much you really loved that ride. I just happen to be the owner and so . . . just for you . . ." he paused and then raised his arm to that prepubescent ride attendant. "One more time!" he yelled.

Where had he come from?

To my horror, we were strapped back in as the ride began again. My daughter and her friend were laughing their heads off as unobtrusively as possible and the owner behind me was doing more than his own fair share of chuckling too. This time around, I spent the ride not only planning my own funeral but with malicious delight, that of my daughter and the devil sitting behind us.

With wobbly knees and shaking hands, I crawled off and onto the wonderful, solid ground when the ride ended. As I turned to my daughter to let her know that I'd never, ever trust her judgment again—and that the rest of my week would be spent dreaming up an appropriate punishment for what she gleefully put me through—I saw the happiness shining in her eyes. And was that . . . could it be . . . perhaps a touch of pride?

"Good job, Mom," she whispered softly.

A quick squeeze on my arm and she was off to ogle the boys and go on more horrifying rides. The fear, the panic melted away. I realized that I had indeed strengthened our bond and created a memory. For that brief, shining moment I knew in my heart that mothers and teenage daughters truly could reach out now and then and be friends.

TAMRA B. ORR

VI
FROM SHIFTING SAND
TO SOLID GROUND

The need for change bulldozed
a road down the center of my mind.

MAYA ANGELOU

PRACTICE MAKES PERFECT

The summer before we started high school, my best friend, Kathy, joined the school band and started going to band practice every Tuesday and Thursday night.

"But you don't play an instrument," I pointed out. "How can you be in the band?"

"It's actually called band front," she explained. "We twirl flags while the band plays." Then her eyes lit up. "Hey! You could come with me next week. You've only missed a few practices. We'll have so much fun!"

I laughed. "Fun? Me? Twirling a flag?"

Over the next few days, I thought about it a lot. On the one hand, I knew nothing about twirling flags and didn't want to make a fool of myself. But on the other hand, I already knew Kathy and I wouldn't have any of the same classes when school started, and this would be something we could do together. Plus, I had gone to a different junior high school than everyone else and I didn't know many people. "This would be a good chance to make some new friends," my parents said, adding their voices to Kathy's when she told me. "They travel all over for competitions and they go on trips! It'll be great!"

The next Tuesday night, I succumbed to the pressure and went to band practice.

"This is my friend, Carol," Kathy announced to the instructor and the twenty or so other flag twirlers. "She wants to join."

I wanted to argue that I never said I'd join—that I had just agreed to give it a try, but I was too nervous to say anything. Then everyone started doing these spins with their flags while the instructor came over to teach me a few moves. Since I was exactly five feet tall and clumsy, twirling a flag didn't come easy for me. During the next several practices, I dropped the flag constantly. I jammed it into the ground while trying to spin it. I hit myself in the shins. I hit myself in the head. I hit Kathy in the head. I thought I'd never get it.

But I loved it, and I really wanted to learn how to do all those fancy spins and twirls. So I kept going to practice, and I finally stopped dropping the flag and hitting people with it. I was thrilled when Kathy's dad surprised us with two flags he had made out of wooden poles with sheets attached to them. I'm sure we gave her neighbors a lot of laughs as we marched up and down the street for hours twirling our homemade flags.

When school started, we had three hours of practice each day to prepare for our first parade. The bands would be judged, and our band had won first prize for several years. Wanting to be perfect for the judges, Kathy and I spent our weekends parading around our neighborhoods polishing our routine.

When practice ended on the day before the parade, the band director thanked all of us for our hard work and said what a great job everyone was doing. "We're gonna go get 'em tomorrow!" he announced, and everyone cheered. I was so happy I was almost crying. I couldn't wait for the parade! I went into the band room to put my flag away, and the director asked if he could see me in his office. "Sure," I replied, thinking he wanted to congratulate me on my brilliant twirling. When I entered his office, another girl was there, too. The director told us both that he knew how hard we had worked and he wanted us to be in the parade. But when it was our band's turn to perform for the judges, we would be taken out.

I was stunned. *I'm not good enough for the judges?* I thought, and I fought back my tears. I left the school without a word, got into my mother's car, and started crying so hard that I couldn't even tell her what was wrong. Finally, I managed to get the words out and told her what the director had said and that I was quitting.

"Then let's go back and you can tell him you're quitting," she said.

"I'm not going back there!" I told her. "I just won't show up tomorrow, and I'll never go to practice again, and sooner or later he'll figure out that I quit."

My mother had already turned the car around and was heading toward the school.

"If you're going to quit, you're going to quit in person," she said.

"Fine!" I huffed, as I got out of the car and slammed the door. "I'll go in there and quit, and I'll tell him exactly what I think of him, too!"

But my courage faded as I entered the band room, and I was ready to turn around and run back out when I heard, "Carol, what can I do for you?"

The band director was standing there, giving me a big smile.

"I'm quitting," I managed to squeak out, almost inaudibly, as a tear escaped from my eye.

He put his arm around me and led me to his tiny office. "I wish you wouldn't," he said.

I was confused. "What do you mean, you wish I wouldn't? I'm not even good enough to be in the parade tomorrow."

Then he told me how much fun it looked like I was having at practice, and how much potential I had. "You're not ready to go in front of the judges just yet," he said. "But if you keep working, you will be . . . very soon."

The next day, I marched with the band through the whole parade. Every time we did our routine for the crowd and heard the applause, I was so proud. And when we were approaching the judging stand, I felt a tap on my shoulder and knew it was time to move over to the sidewalk.

When the parade was over, the director came over to me.

"You did great out there today," he said, "and I'm really proud of you."

The following Monday, the band got to work on our "field show," the routines we would do for football-game halftime shows and competitions. I figured that when it came time to assign everyone a spot, I would again be left out. I don't know whether I was more thrilled or more shocked to find that there was a permanent spot for me.

I performed for the judges at every competition that season and for the next three seasons until I graduated high school. Although I loved every minute of it, two moments stand out: being named flag captain at the beginning of my senior year, and being named best flag at the band banquet ending my senior year. As I hugged our band director after the banquet, I thanked him for the award.

"I'm just glad you didn't quit," he said.

And so was I.

CAROL SJOSTROM MILLER

Without discipline, there is no life at all.
KATHARINE HEPBURN

SCALING NEW HEIGHTS

I have to tell you the God's honest truth. Four years ago, my scale had been my worst enemy, always giving me the three-digit number 185 on my four-foot-eight frame. Always driving me to kick it, stub my toe, hop up and down, then fall to my knees crying because I couldn't lose any weight.

I remember my dad yelling at me, "Mary, you have to lose weight! You're fatter than me!"

He took away all my favorite foods—potato chips, cookies, and gallons of coffee ice cream. My heart twisted and my stomach churned. I wanted to eat and still be thin and pretty like all those gorgeous models with the sparkling white teeth, skimpy outfits, long legs, and flat tummies—the ones in *Seventeen*, *Teen People*, and *Vogue*.

My dad wasn't the worst. Each month I'd tell my cousin, "I'm on a diet." She'd roll her eyes and say, "Again?"

I remember my relatives eyeing me with pity, shaking their heads. I could read their minds without even trying. *Poor Mary. When is she going to lose weight?*

It was more than I could take. Relatives pitying me. Thin models prancing in front of me. Dad scolding me. I knew I had to do something. I thought back to those TV commercials saying things like, "You can lose more weight than ever . . . Pay twenty dollars to lose more than seventy-eight pounds and you do absolutely nothing . . . I lost more than fifty pounds in six months . . ."

Before-and-after pictures flashed in front of me. The commercials plagued me. I snapped off the tube. It was time to lose weight *my* way. I set a goal of 116 pounds. I told my family and they laughed.

I was a freshman in high school when I made a chart that listed "Time," "Date," and "Weight." I took an old notebook and labeled it "Food Diary" and jotted down the food and calories I consumed every single day. Instead of using the white-and-blue porcelain bowl in which I used to pile meat onto a Mount Everest of rice, I used a plate where I divided up all the food equally. I exercised on the stationary bicycle for fifteen minutes at first. Sweat dripped down my body as I struggled to catch my breath. Two months later, fifteen minutes turned into twenty, then into thirty. I wasn't as tired as before. In fact, I was barely sweating.

I did this every single day. Every single burning, aching, heart-wrenching day. Here was my routine. Breakfast: cereal with 2 percent low-fat milk. Lunch: turkey sandwich and crackers. Thirty minutes of biking in front of *Days of Our Lives*. Dinner: rice, veggies, and a slab of meat. At times I hated the monotony of it. Oh yeah, I was losing weight slowly but steadily. My chart proved that, yet I could still see my double chin, and I still disliked shopping. Squeezing into an extra-large size was an accomplishment, considering it had been all plus sizes for "Fat Mary," but it wasn't enough. I wanted more. I wanted to fit into jeans and tank tops. I had to keep going. I couldn't give up when I was so close.

It wasn't until college—when I went swimming at the gym and walked around the campus three times with so little effort—that I came to love the scale. The scale I'd despised four years earlier grinned the numbers 130, then 120.

When relatives and friends see me, they're amazed, shocked, bewildered, and baffled. They ask how I lost all that weight. I shrug and say that all you need in order to lose weight are three things: determination, self-control, and most of all, patience. I knew how to lose weight all along, which is hard in a society that values the quicker-is-better principle, shorter lines, e-mails, microwaves, and McDonald's—but guess what? There's no quick way to the things that really matter most.

Today I step on to the scale, take a deep breath, let it all out, and smile. My scale is my new best friend. In my chart, I write the date, time, and weight, and stand there, with red pen in hand, staring off into space: 116 pounds! From 185 pounds to 116 pounds. I can't believe it: 116 pounds!

Mountaineers spend lifetimes scaling peaks and I'd managed to scale my way up to 185 pounds and turned myself into a mountain of a girl with so little effort. On *National Geographic* specials, the announcer usually says how it takes a certain kind of person to climb mountains. The focus is always on the climb, never the descent. What I've learned is that the trip down is just as rigorous as the ascent—often fraught with sags in spirit, rubbery legs, and hunger. Yet, all good things come with time. Determination and an eye on the goal brought me back to base camp.

Now is the time for celebration as I greet the new me—someone I've longed to see for a very long time.

MARY H. WU

PLASTIC CURTAINS

*T**he clear plastic curtains in our upstairs apart-*
ment living room came from the five-and-dime and
were decorated with huge pink painted roses. These
window coverings reached from ceiling to floor. Sunshine filtered
through pink plastic flowers was gaudy hot in all seasons. Late afternoons glowed, became a hushed melon color, but nights took
on a ghostlike pallor when the moon rose over the Mississippi.

I missed our other house's sleek hardwood floors and chande-
liers. That was the "before Daddy left house." My mother rented
the apartment when my sister entered college and my father re-
married.

Mama said, "We'll rent out the big house and live in a place we
can afford."

The upstairs apartment was in a 1920 brick building with a
backyard that overlooked the Mississippi River. We had a private
entrance, a long flight of stairs, living room, kitchen, two bed-
rooms, bath, and an upstairs back porch.

At our other house my parents played Strauss waltzes. Here, I
preferred Joni James and Nat King Cole. When I liked a song I
played it over and over. I liked "Oh Happy Day" after we moved
into the apartment. Harold, the current man in my mother's life,
hated that song.

"That isn't music," he roared. "Why do you let her play that
trash, Hildegarde?"

My mother walked over to the record player, lifted my record
off, and put on Glenn Miller. Harold played trumpet in a band

across the river in Illinois at The Purple Crackle. He had a sandy-colored mustache and drove a black Ford. He wasn't divorced like my mother. Harold's wife of many years died after a lingering illness and left him, his trumpet, one son, and a dog. The dog wore a curled lip. The kid was a drip. I didn't speak to him at school. The idea that we might become a family made me hot all over, perspire, and chill at the same time. My legs became pogo sticks. There was no escape when I thought about family.

My bedroom had twin beds and a gray dresser. The headboards for the beds leaned against magnolia flower wallpaper. My mother and I didn't have much luck hooking them on to the metal bed frames. The wool rug lay rolled up in front of a tower of moving boxes in the corner. My stuff seemed safest left in boxes, since there was no closet in this room.

At night, cars tossed bold reflections into my bedroom windows. I pulled blankets over my head to meet the black night. Grandmother's quilts covered both beds. I missed them both, my grandmother and my sister. Sophia Newcomb was the college my father and his new wife picked for my sister to study French and political science. She was dating a boy whose father owned a coffee plantation. I marked on my calendar the days until Christmas, when my sister would come home with a trunk full of New Orleans clothes, strapless gowns, cashmere sweaters, and tweed skirts, clothes I could borrow.

One Friday night, I went to the high-school football game. Friends dropped me off afterward. It was almost eleven when I got home. At the top of the stairs I hesitated. I heard soft music. My palms grew damp. I strained to listen, and opened the door. The only light in the room came from a lamp on the end table. Two drinking glasses pooled water next to an ashtray with cigarette butts. Harold smoked Kents. My mother didn't smoke. It was obvious. Harold was here again. I knew they must be out in the kitchen drinking coffee and eating my mother's angel food cake. I coughed and walked into the kitchen, where my mother stood at the sink rinsing something. Her black hair looked a little tousled, and her Merle Norman lipstick was gone. The back porch door stood ajar. I guessed that Harold was on the back porch. *All right, I can wait you out, Harold.*

I sat down on a chrome kitchen chair. A package of Kents lay open on the table. Minutes froze on the kitchen clock before a red-faced Harold came in from the porch. He ran his hands through his hair and wiped his mouth with a handkerchief. I saw signs of my mother's Watermelon Red lipstick. I stared until his squinted eyes met mine. Out of frustration, I didn't know what else to do, so I reached across the table and took his package of cigarettes. I popped one out of the pack the way I had practiced and tapped it on the back of my hand. I placed it between my lips and raised his lighter. Harold watched me draw the smoke in and exhale it into his direction. A muscle in his cheek twitched. I coughed. My mother's back was turned. There were no words between the three of us, only the smoke, which curled in the air, rose to the ceiling, and disappeared.

I felt furious with my mother for starting a romance. I wanted my father's feather kisses touching her face, not Harold's.

Harold spoke of leaving. My mother followed him into the living room. I listened to muffled words, their silence. Imagined more kissing. My eyes burned before tears gathered in the corners. I snubbed out the cigarette and went to bed.

Several weeks later my mother traveled to St. Louis on business for her job at the army recruiting office. She decided that at sixteen I was old enough to stay at home without her for one week. She did our hand wash of lingerie on Sunday and hung it on the backyard line before she left.

"Don't forget to bring in our clothes," she reminded me.

Night dragged after my mother left. In the evening I turned on all of the lights and played a stack of records. I did geometry homework and went to bed after rolling my hair in rag rollers. I listened to cars passing the house. River barges announced their presence with foghorns as they moved south in the night. I slept with a stuffed bear guarding my back. In the morning before school I fixed myself a decent breakfast—buttered toast, scrambled eggs. I doctored the Folgers with half a cup of milk.

Monday night my boyfriend, Paul Wayne, called on the telephone. He wanted to come over to study with me, but I knew how my mother would frown on my entertaining Paul when she was gone.

"Paul, you know my mom would have a fit if you came over while she's out of town. She trusts me not to have boys in the house when she's away. Let's do our biology homework over the phone."

He grumbled at first but accepted my suggestion. After the homework we talked about going to the football game on Friday night.

After I hung up the phone, I thought about Paul, with his dark hair and hazel eyes. He always smelled like Wrigley's gum and Ivory soap. He and my father were very different. My father wore Old Spice and moved around in the world with urgency. Paul Wayne was shy with an impish grin and sauntered. He didn't seem to be in a hurry to prove anything. I felt relaxed with him. I could be me.

When I thought about my father, I thought about his leaving. And that my mom was now dating—all a daunting reminder that my parents would never be together again. What did my mother see in Harold? Surely she would come to her senses regarding him.

Before getting ready for bed I went into my mother's bedroom. It was dark and cool, and it seemed lonely without her here. I turned on her bedside lamp, opened her maple bureau drawer, and lifted out her rose-colored cashmere sweater. I knew she wouldn't mind if I borrowed it. Maybe I could wear it on my date with Paul on Friday. The sweater felt soft. The color was splendid. My grandmother always told me shades of rose or pink looked good on me with my blonde hair. I was fair like all of my father's family. I put the sweater away and returned to the living room. There was no lamplight now. The moon looked into the window through painted roses on the plastic curtains.

When my mother returned, she was angry to find that I had forgotten to bring in the hand wash all week while she was away. Our panties, bras, and slips were harsh, stiff, and faded from the winter weather. They hung firmly pinned on the revolving clothesline, their delicate softness lost forever. They never were the same, but we wore them anyway.

Harold eventually moved to Texas, and my first important boyfriend, Paul, joined the army and went to Korea after someone in my mother's office recruited him. I gradually grew accustomed to the plastic curtains in the living room as the sun faded the flowers and offered me a better view of the river from the window. There were always seasonal changes on the river, but the thing I missed most when I went off to college was the sound of the riverboat foghorns passing our home in the night.

JUDITH BADER JONES

MY UNKISSED SELF

*T*he expression *"Sweet sixteen and never been kissed"* was too close to reality for me during my third year of high school. Technically, I did not qualify for that label because of one unexpected lip lock at overnight camp with a boy I hardly knew and, worse, didn't want to know. Deep down, though, I still felt unkissed. My teenage intuition told me that a kiss should have an emotional component, and mine did not.

Each time one of my girlfriends went out on a date, I felt jealous and confused. What was wrong with me? I talked and laughed with lots of boys in my classes. I was reasonably smart, but not so smart as to be intimidating. And I was at least as attractive as my friends were, in a late-sixties, straightened-hair, padded-bra sort of way.

Why did the boys notice me enough to talk to me at school, but not enough to phone me for a date? So I read romance novels, memorized lines from the film *Romeo and Juliet,* and babysat on Saturday nights, fantasizing about the day when the real kiss would happen.

By the time I was a seventeen-year-old high-school senior, I had lost all hope of finding a date from among the boys in my school. I also seriously questioned the existence of another boy anywhere in the universe who would ever kiss me.

I had first met David in junior high. As above-average students, we were in and out of classes together throughout the next five years. Then as seniors, we ended up seated beside each other in calculus. I had always done fairly well in math, but this subject was giving me trouble. Eventually we became study partners, which led to several phone calls each week.

Over a period of months, we started discussing other things about our lives once we'd finished the math problems. I found out he was a jazz pianist. And that he dreamed of riding a raft down the Mississippi River like Huck Finn. I'd had similar dreams myself. Our conversations became more and more important to me, but I tempered my excitement with the knowledge that he was only calling because of the homework.

One Monday after we'd finished the "math" portion of our call, he asked what I was doing on Friday night. My typical Friday evening consisted of reading, watching TV, or talking on the phone to my only other girlfriend who didn't date. He wanted to take me to a movie: a French film showing at a small local theater. I said great, and he said he'd let me know later in the week about the time.

As soon as we hung up, I ran straight to my room and collapsed onto the bed. I rolled around in small convulsions of tears and laughter. Quietly, though, because I didn't want to alert my family. I wasn't going to tell anyone yet. Not even my best friend Marilyn. What if I had imagined the entire conversation? I was still haunted by an incident during junior high school that had made me doubt my ability to hear what boys were saying to me. Larry, a cute redhead from my seventh-grade science class with whom I had been flirting, suddenly blurted out, "Wanna go steady?" The next day, he acted like nothing had happened. In fact, I don't think we spoke to each other again. As I reflected on the experience years later, I could not recall my response to his proposal. Had I said yes, or had I run screaming from the room? Either way, it reinforced my opinion that males could act interested in me one minute and totally erase me from their life the next.

I fought to keep a lid on my anxiety, while telling myself that given everything David had shared with me, he couldn't back out now. That got me through Tuesday. By Wednesday, when he hadn't brought up the subject of the movie, I began to panic. I knew his invitation had been real, but I was too terrified to mention it in class. I phoned Marilyn and spilled the whole story, swearing her to secrecy. She said he'd probably finalize the date the next day; I didn't know if I'd live to the next day. I did, and her prediction came true.

At the movies on Friday evening, David and I sat shoulder to shoulder, with the occasional knee brushing against knee. He held my hand intermittently, letting go when it felt too sweaty and then shifting his arm around the back of my seat. All of this touching and near touching distracted me from reading the subtitles. Even if it hadn't been in French, I could not follow the film's plot because I was focused on our postmovie plot possibilities. I wondered, *How will this end? Will we kiss on my doorstep?*

Afterward he asked if I needed to go straight home. I said I didn't, so he drove to a secluded spot and we got out of the car to look at the constellations. The early spring night was cold and damp; we could see our breath. He pulled me close and we kissed. I felt warm inside and leaned in for more.

Two hours later, I lay in bed replaying each detail of the evening, fingertips at my face, lightly tracing the lips that were no longer only mine. My unkissed self was a different girl now—a kissed girl—and I knew that the greatest adventures in my life were just beginning.

MARILYN D. DAVIS

ONE LICK AT A TIME

I tossed a bag of Tootsie Pops on top of my small mound of camping gear. Picking up the bag, I bit a hole through the plastic and slipped two Tootsie Pops into my pocket. Slowly, I turned to survey my new set of Burnamwood campers and quickly focused on one girl sitting apart from the others.

"Angel?" I called.

"Yes, ma'am."

"You're going to climb Old Baldy."

"No, ma'am. I ain't." Angel, a feisty thirteen-year-old with hair the color of sunburned poppies, scuffed her tennis shoes (two sizes too big) against the dirt. A cloud of hot, mustard-yellow dust rose.

I casually unwrapped a Tootsie Pop.

"It's not that I won't, ma'am. It's that I can't." Angel snapped the watermelon bubble gum, blew an enormous bubble, and popped it with her finger.

"What—no mountains in Duvall?" The words, tossed like a basketball bouncing off sizzling hot asphalt on an inner-city playground, came from a tall mountain boy. He dribbled a ball on a small slab of concrete at the edge of the mountain. Then he threw it to another boy with a shock of orange hair, who went up for a shot. The ball hit the backboard and slipped through the torn net. The tall boy spat into his hand, "No offense, Duvall."

The word *Duvall* stuck in the air. The other campers (teenagers with shoes that fit) stared at the girl with cinnamon eyes. Angel stared hard at her dirty, unlaced tennis shoes. She was large for her age and her heavy makeup, like a mask worn over another mask, concealed a pretty, pale, innocent face. Hurting. Like a wildflower growing up in hard earth, Angel wore an expression too old for one so young. As she pulled the black jacket tight around her, Angel seemed almost to shrink, disappearing inside her black T-shirt with the words NO FEAR printed in white across the back. The lettering was cracked.

Sunlight glinted off her baseball cap, turned inside out and wrong side in. She might have cried but the tears had dried up. So instead, she twisted a piece of wild licorice grass around fingers. Fingers that knew how to "borrow" lipstick and deep purple fingernail polish and watermelon bubble gum but knew nothing about holding on to a rope while climbing a mountain.

Angel felt my hand on her shoulder: "You're in charge of the s'mores." I pressed chocolate bars, graham crackers, and marshmallows into her callused hand and nodded to the others. "Ya'll go on. We'll catch up."

The other counselor and campers headed toward the trail. Angel didn't budge. "I thought this was a Christian sports camp."

"It is."

"Climbing a mountain isn't a sport. There's no players, no teams."

"There's you. And the mountain." I held out the candy. "Angel, how do you eat a Tootsie Pop?"

"You lick it."

"Show me."

Suspicious, she licked the candy. Cherry juice bubbled around the corners of her mouth.

"You don't just bite down hard?"

"No, ma'am. It's too hard. Might break a tooth."

"You lick it slowly. Till you get to the chocolate center?"

"Are we going somewhere with all this?"

"We're going to the top of Old Baldy. One lick at a time."

I took off. And Angel followed up through windblown wild grass, and at the foot of the trail, she whispered, "When we get to the top, could I have another Tootsie Pop?"

"What flavor?"

"Grape."

Together, we climbed to the first bend where wild violets grew. *The first lick!* Then, we followed the steep trail to a log bridge, where we gazed up at clouds that shaped themselves into strings of pearls and glittering jewels, rhinestone shoes . . . ice cream cones and Tootsie Pops. *The second lick!*

Dusk tiptoed close behind.

Angel and I climbed higher. Then, surprisingly, the path opened into a meadow covered in wildflowers. Angel held out her hand and a monarch butterfly lit on the tip of her finger . . . until she sneezed and it disappeared! *Another lick!*

The last stretch curled down, then up, sharply. And the top of Old Baldy disappeared beneath a canopy of pine. Catching our breath, we rested on tangled roots of a sycamore tree.

"Nobody pushed me."

The secret spilled out, like small sips of air. "It just got slippery, because of the sudden rain. My mama said it was a gum tree, with real gumballs. So I climbed up real high but my foot caught and I went sliding back down, upside down."

I sat real still, listening to my breathing.

"I caught on, ya know, that there aren't any magical gumball trees. Not in Duvall Housing Project. There's just ordinary trees and wishing won't make gumballs grow on a plain old maple tree."

She took off her hat. The mountain wind blew soft and cool across her bare face; the climb had melted the makeup. Her eyes were pools of light.

"Later on, my mama left and then I ran away too. Far away, deep inside me to a secret place that's real dark. Where there's just me and a pocketful of stolen gumballs."

"Your mother came back, Angel."

"She came back too late." The young girl brushed her hand across her eyes and then she cried. Quietly, she emptied her pocket of brightly colored gumballs, which fell across the tree roots as if they *had* fallen from the branches of the majestic white-barked tree. I gathered the gumballs and pressed them into Angel's hand.

"Don't ever stop believing, Angel. When you can see something with your heart, then it is real. It's the believing that gives us the courage to climb our gumball trees."

Angel popped a gumball in her mouth, blew a bubble, and grinned.

Another lick!

At last we reached a hollow log propped up against a smooth limestone wall and, with faces smudged and jeans torn, we climbed to the top of the mountain. Angel raced ahead to the edge and gazed out over the treetops, guardian angel of her own mountain. Then she did a beautiful thing. She held out her arms as if she were about to fly. And some part of her did fly—her spirit soared.

I hugged her and gave her the grape Tootsie Pop. We heard footsteps, and the tall mountain boy appeared. "Ya made it. Awesome."

Angel unwrapped the candy. "It was easy . . . like licking a Tootsie Pop."

MARGARET C. PRICE

Certainly, travel is more than the seeing of sights;
it is a change that goes on, deep and permanent, in the ideas of living.
MIRIAM BEARD

THE GRASS IS ALWAYS GREENER

*I*dreaded returning to school after Christmas break. Not because I hated my classes or teachers, but because I knew I would once again be subjected to the annual postholiday gloating of Mary and Lisa, the rich sisters. When they changed into their gym suits for PE, they were instantly surrounded by a gaggle of girls admiring their deep and glorious tans.

Every year they went to Florida for the holidays then played it cool as each classmate held a ghostly white arm next to one of theirs for a masochistic comparison. The pale shade of green I wore was not very pretty beside sun-kissed brown. What made it worse was how nonchalant they were, as if they'd simply gone three towns over. Which was pretty much all my family did as we made the rounds of our relatives' homes. They all lived in Missouri. I'd never been anywhere.

I was twelve years old for goodness' sake. By the time Laura Ingalls was twelve, she'd been through a whole bunch of states. Sure she settled in Missouri when she was grown up and married, but that was after she'd traveled all over the place. And she did it in a covered wagon. We had a car. You'd think we could go some-where. Anywhere besides the "State of Misery." Our map re-vealed that we had our very own Mexico, Cairo, Lebanon, Glasgow, and Grenada in the "Show Me State." But show me one of these intriguingly named places, and I could show you just an-other Midwestern town with the same old four seasons year in and year out, same old rolling hills, same old trees and bluffs.

Mom must have overheard me lamenting our static existence to my brother and sister in the back seat as she drove us from Jackson to "the city" (Cape Girardeau) to see a movie, because af-terward she gaily asked if we'd like to cross the state line into Illi-nois. Her question was met with a stunned silence. We could do that? Were we really that close to the Land of Lincoln? Wouldn't there be guards or something? Didn't we need special passes? I couldn't speak, but fortunately my little brother and sister cho-rused a yes, and bounced up and down in their seats with excite-ment.

A few minutes later we were on a bridge crossing the Missis-sippi River. Was this the same bridge our stepfather had told the story about when his car had slid on the ice and gone over into the river and he'd only been saved by holding on to a chunk of ice until he was close enough to the bank to swim? But wait, he'd also told us he couldn't swim just last summer when we'd begged him to go to the pool with us. Plus, this bridge had rails. A car couldn't just slide off the edge. Hmm. I pondered these inconsistencies and tapped a finger on the door handle to the *thunk-thunk-thunk* of our tires rolling over the sectioned concrete. Well, anyway, this was the Mighty Mississippi, and it was definitely the one Tom Sawyer and Huck Finn had spent so much time on and in, and here I was, zooming right over it.

When we got across the bridge, I was a bit disappointed to dis-cover that it didn't look any different from home. Hills, trees, win-ter. Nothing new here. Well, there was that sign I'd never seen before: WELCOME TO ILLINOIS. My heart gave a little jump. Didn't this make me cosmopolitan or continental or something? We all cheered, and Mom made a U-turn.

On our way back to Jackson, we made our usual stop at the cemetery. We didn't know anyone buried there, but at the entrance was a pen that housed a small flock of peacocks. Mom fished a quarter out of her purse, so we could buy a handful of feed pellets out of the machine. We usually fought over who had the most and how unfair life was, but this time I felt too grown-up and too appreciative of my mother to get into an immature rivalry with my siblings. I divided the treats evenly between them, then stood aloof as they tossed them through the chicken wire to the exotic birds.

Back at school, when the sisters flashed their new tans and divulged the secret of lemon juice to get blonde streaks in their hair, I had the good sense to keep quiet. No way could Illinois measure up to Florida. But I had finally been somewhere, and in my heart I knew my future held more distant horizons.

Three years later, in one of those funny little twists of fate, we moved to Florida, where I still live today. I have traveled through much of the United States and Canada and have even been to Europe a couple of times. Yet when I think of Missouri, I feel a pull on my heart. I miss that brown river, those rolling hills, and those tree-shaded bluffs. And I realize that where I grew up was somewhere after all. Somewhere just fine.

APRIL BURK

VII
YOU ARE NEVER ALONE

When you respond to something because it's so beautiful,
you're really looking at the soul
of the person who made it.

ALICE WALKER

THE WITCH AND
HER MAGIC POTION

I *was living in my homeland, Hungary, in a village called* Mosorin in 1943 when I was a young woman. Mosorin was right on the Serbian border, and both Hungarians and Serbians lived there. My grandparents, who were raising me, owned the only general store in town. My grandmother ran the store while Grandfather, the town's judge, attended to his duties at the courthouse.

There was an ancient Serbian woman in Mosorin named Tekla who lived in a shanty at the edge of town. The children of the town were terrified yet strangely fascinated by Tekla. People said she was a witch and that she had strange powers and could put curses on people who made her mad. They also said she made powerful potions and chanted strange-sounding chants, and everyone knew that her only friend was her black cat.

One day, about two weeks before Christmas, I was in the store by myself while Grandma ran up to the courthouse to take Grandfather his lunch. (I didn't go along because it was pouring rain outside.) My nose was buried in a book, while my orange tabby cat, Paprika, snoozed under the counter. Suddenly the front door opened, and in came none other than our resident witch!

Frozen with fright, I stared at her while my curious cat got up and walked around the counter to greet the visitor.

"Hello there, kitty," the old woman crooned in a high-pitched voice. "What a pretty kitty you are." Paprika purred loudly in response, rubbing himself against the old woman.

I was still behind the counter, but the fright slowly subsided as I watched the scenario in front of me.

"I love cats," Tekla said, looking toward me. "They love you for yourself, in spite of the mean things people say about you."

She sounded sad as she said that, so I picked up a hard candy from the jar on the counter, and walked over and offered it to her.

"Thank you," she said, as her bony fingers took the candy from my hand.

By the time Grandma returned, Tekla and I had struck up a friendship.

"I have told you that she wasn't a witch. She is just an odd old woman who lives differently from most people, so they call her a witch," Grandma said after Tekla left.

On Christmas Eve morning, my grandparents and I went to visit a relative in the country. While the adults were busy in the house, I stayed outside and got reacquainted with the resident animals. After a while, I came to the stone steps leading into a cellar. There, I discovered something forbidden—fermenting wine filling the air with a sweet, musk scent from some barrels lined up like soldiers.

One of the barrels had a long, tubelike object conveniently on top of it. I pushed it into the barrel and sucked up the sweet liquid, smacking my lips in appreciation. Then I sucked up some more of it—and more still. Soon my world began to spin, and then everything went black!

When I opened my eyes again, I realized I was back in my own bed. I could hear people talking to each other in hushed voices while my grandmother wailed pitifully somewhere in the room.

"She is in a coma, brought on by alcohol poisoning," a voice I recognized as our doctor was saying. "And she is not responding to treatment."

"Someone go and get the priest!" Grandma wailed. "I don't want her to die without the last sacrament."

I suddenly realized they were talking about me, and tried to sit up. But I couldn't move or talk. I was imprisoned in my own body! Then I lost consciousness again.

I was told later what happened next. It seems that Tekla heard the news that I was dying, so she hurried to our home carrying something. When she knocked at the back door and Grandfather saw her standing there, he almost closed the door in her face.

"I have a potion. It will help your granddaughter get well," Tekla said loudly.

"Go away, old woman," Grandfather told her gruffly, but Grandma came to the door to see who it was.

Tekla told her about the potion, and added, "I know it will help her."

So my desperate grandmother took the jar containing the dark liquid and—despite the objections of the doctor—administered it to me on the spot.

"It wasn't easy to get it into your mouth," she later told me. "We had to pry your mouth open and spoon it in slowly. Then we laid you down again and began a prayer vigil at your bedside."

The following dawn, which was Christmas Day, I opened my eyes. I heard murmuring in the room and realized people were praying. Then I heard Grandma crying softly somewhere nearby. I turned my head to see if I could see her and realized I could move! I wiggled my fingers and toes. They all seemed to be working again! But what was that strange feeling in the pit of my stomach?

Then, recognizing the feeling, I suddenly sat up and cried out, "Grandma, where are you? I'm sooo hungry!"

"It's a miracle!" someone in the room shouted, as Grandma ran to my side.

"It's Tekla's potion," Grandma said joyously. "It worked just as she said it would."

Grandma moved me into the parlor then, where a beautiful Christmas tree was already ablaze with candles. She plucked a star-shaped honey cookie from the tree, and handed it to me, and I devoured it and wanted another one! Soon I was opening my presents, which were mainly homemade items, except for a special book, and as I sat reading the book, Grandma cooked our Christmas dinner, a roast goose. Meanwhile, Grandfather went with the wagon to fetch a special guest for dinner—Tekla.

"Did you really give me a magic potion, like everyone says you did?" I asked her after dinner.

"Everyone says my potions are magic, but to me they are only old formulas taught to me by my dear, departed papa. They are made with herbs and barks of trees and such," Tekla replied, giving me an almost toothless smile. "Because of these formulas, I have grown very old without ever seeing a doctor. And now, one of them helped you get well, so I guess they really must be magic."

A few weeks later, Tito's communist partisans were gaining on the region, so my grandparents and I left Mosorin for good, moving into upper Hungary. I never saw Tekla the "witch" again, but I have never forgotten how she saved my life with her magic potion.

And I've never had a drop of alcohol since!

RENIE SZILAK BURGHARDT

My diary seems to keep me whole.
ANAÏS NIN

GROWING PAINS

My daughter Nikki came downstairs, holding an
atlas, her face streaked with tears. I knew why she
was crying. Her friend Maggie was moving to another state.

"I'll never see Maggie again," Nikki said as her finger traced the
route across the map to Maggie's new home. I wanted to tell her
that they'd visit, but I knew it wasn't likely.

"Oh, Nikki, I know this is hard," I said.

My words sounded hollow, useless. I followed her as she ran to
her room, shutting the door behind her. Unbidden, a childhood
memory came to me, a memory of my first broken heart, when I
ran into my room, ignoring the hand my mother tried to offer me.
But my grief was powerful. I had to talk to someone so I turned to
a pink-and-white book I hid in my sock drawer—my diary.

At the time, my family lived on a one-acre dusty patch of land
in rural Arizona. We had recently moved from a home in Virginia,
a home surrounded by maple trees, with a familiar bedroom, and
most important, near best friends. After we moved, my four sisters ran around outside, chasing tumbleweeds. They each baked
their skin to a golden brown under the ever-present Arizona sun. I
didn't share their enthusiasm. I stayed inside, reading and writing

letters to the friends I'd left behind. I was lost and lonely, and not enamored with desert life.

One day a kid named Jimmy, who was sitting behind me on the school bus, started tugging on my shirt.

"Kelly, want to see some puppies?" he asked. Jimmy had tried to be friends with me ever since we moved here, but I wasn't interested. He talked too much, mostly about The Thing or Mr. Fantastic from some weird cartoon show. But this time he'd said something interesting. I listened.

"Where?" I asked.

"At my house. Come on," he said as I followed him down the dirt road. Behind his house, lying under the shade of a lone tree, I saw tiny mounds of fur nuzzling the belly of a big black dog. Then I noticed another puppy, lying off to the side.

"Why isn't the mom feeding this one?" I asked.

"That's the runt. He'll never live," Jimmy said as he kicked a pile of dirt.

"What do you mean he'll never live? What are you going to do to him?" I scooped the puppy up into my arms.

"We'll just leave him alone. Runts usually die on their own. You know, nature and all that."

I hesitated, thinking about what my mother would say if I brought a puppy home. But I couldn't trust Jimmy.

"Can I have him?" I asked.

"Go ahead. Don't know why you'd want that scrawny puppy." Before Jimmy could say any more, I ran home and begged my mom to keep him. Mom tried to resist, but she caved, unable to turn away a small, helpless dog. When my sisters came home, they crowded around me, trying to pry the puppy from my arms. I wasn't about to let go.

"It's a boy," I told them. "I named him Duro. It means tough in Spanish. Any helpless creature that makes it alive out of Jimmy's house is tough." And so Duro became a permanent member of our family. We all vied for ownership of Duro.

"It's not fair! I never get anything of my own," we whined. It was true. Singular ownership of any one thing in our family was next to impossible. We showered Duro with attention, and rushed to feed him, hoping to sway his allegiance in one direction. The novelty wore off, though, and my sisters lost interest. Not me. I continued to take care of Duro. Slowly, it dawned on my sisters that Duro was ignoring them.

"That's not a family pet. Kelly's hogging him!" they complained. They were right. Duro had snubbed everyone except me. He became my buddy, my shadow, trotting behind me everywhere I went. I set up a playpen for him, in front of our family-room window. When I went to school in the morning, Duro stood up in the playpen, placed his front paws on the windowsill. He just stared. I don't think he moved until I became a dot so small he didn't recognize me anymore. And after school, as soon as I turned the corner to my house, I could see Duro's little black nose smashed against the window, as if he'd heard the creaking of the bus door as soon as it opened.

Duro spent most of his time indoors, but on occasion I let him play outside. When I opened the front door, he bounded out, wagging his tail, stopping every few minutes to sniff all the new and unusual wonders in the Wild West of the great outdoors.

One warm summer evening, I let Duro out front to play and went back into the house to watch my sister Kim get ready for a date. I watched Kim brush blue eyeshadow on her lids and spray perfume on her neck. I heard the rumble of a car engine outside the bedroom window. I peeked out the window and watched a truck slow down in front of our house. "He's coming," I said.

"All I can say is that Jeff better open the gate and park in front of our house like I told him to. Last time he sat on the road, honking, waiting for me to come to his beck and call." Kim sprayed one last shot of hairspray on her long blonde hair.

Something about Kim's words didn't sit right with me. Then I remembered. I'd let Duro outside.

"Duro!" I yelled as I ran outside. Just as my sister had hoped, her date had opened the gate and parked his truck right in front of our house. He was leaning over, picking up Duro.

"I'm so sorry, I didn't see anything," Jeff said when he saw me. I grabbed my puppy from him. My family heard the commotion and came outside, crowding around me.

"What happened?" Mom asked.

"I ran over the puppy. I don't know what to say. I had no idea the dog was in front of my truck." Jeff's voice was shaky.

"Oh Kelly," Mom said as she gently scooped Duro out of my arms. I ran into the house, straight to my bedroom. I buried my face in my pillow and recounted the events over and over in my mind, as if by doing so I could change one small detail, make things different. Nothing worked.

A few minutes later, my mom came into my room. She tried to hug me but I pushed her away. When it started to get dark I turned on the light and took my pink-and-white book out of my drawer. I poured my heart into pages of my diary, writing about the life and death of my puppy. Each word eased my pain. Duro lives on in my diary where I wrote about our time together.

I noticed there were no more sounds coming from Nikki's room. I opened the door and saw her lying on the bed, a small book in front of her. She was writing as fast as she could, the words spilling out as her tears had spilled out earlier. I watched her for a moment then left, quietly closing the door behind me, letting Nikki finish her story.

KELLY SCHEUFLER

DRIVING MISS LISA

When I was in grade school, I didn't need to tell my father I hated riding the school bus. Instinctively, he knew I'd rather be with him. Sometimes I rode the bus because I was an optimistic girl, convinced that this day everything would be fine. Given one more chance, no one would say mean things, or flick me on the back of the head. But on the days when I couldn't face the unknown, my father understood. I would sit next to him in the old green truck. He'd smile and say, "Buckle up," and I knew I was safe.

When I became a teenager, I grew up and decided my parents didn't know much about anything. At sixteen I couldn't wait to use my new driver's license. One day while I was begging to drive to school myself, my mouth fell open when I heard Dad say yes. I couldn't believe my good fortune!

I'd begun to think he didn't trust my abilities, or me. On that cold January morning, with my faith restored, I slid behind the wheel of my 1971 Pontiac Catalina, a boat large enough to hold seven more skinny girls just like me. I backed out into the road and glanced in the rearview mirror, and there was my father's Ford truck, following me.

How embarrassing can life get?

I just hoped the parking lot would be empty when our caravan pulled in to school. He stayed with me right up until I pulled in to a designated spot.

I brought my car to a jerky stop, and he watched me get out, rolled down the window of the old truck, and gave me a hearty wave in front of everyone.

Oh, the shame!

The next day Dad followed me to the school entrance but didn't turn in. Yes! My freedom was coming. I could feel it.

After a week, I secretly prayed he'd go straight to work and forget about being my escort service. My hands were glued to the cold steering wheel at the ten and two o'clock positions. I didn't dare fiddle with the radio or he might decide I still wasn't ready to be cut loose entirely. Not far from our house, I checked behind me and there he was. I noticed a little grin on his face barely visible from under the hat he always wore. Like a good driver, I flipped on my blinker, took a deep breath, and turned. After a few seconds, I looked back for a sign of the familiar green truck plodding along behind me. He was gone.

I let out a huge sigh of relief then drew in the smell of fear. What if I do something wrong? Who will help me? I scolded myself—you wanted independence and here it is riding shotgun with you! Suddenly, I felt powerful, invincible, and adult. I relaxed and turned the radio up, loud.

He never followed me to school again because I'd earned his trust. He'd taught me well—I was a safe driver. Most of the time I remembered not to tailgate or speed up at a caution light. With my favorite music blaring, I sang and drove around town, trying to look cool in my big family size car. Sometimes, out of the corner of my eye, I would spot a green Ford truck with white detail stripes on the hood. My mouth would clamp shut. Immediately, I'd turn the volume down of the new song I'd waited all day to hear. I would sit up straight and still, check to make sure my seat belt was fastened, and a loving but stern parental voice in my head would whisper, "Buckle up."

I'd drive by those look-alike trucks with both hands pressed tightly on the steering wheel and hold my breath until they passed me anonymously. But on more than one occasion, I'd see that familiar grin and a see-you-at-supper wave. It was at those moments that I'd feel the most grateful for a father that knew when to pull in the reins and when to release them to let me run free.

LISA KAUFMAN

It's not who you know, it's who knows you!
AUTHOR UNKNOWN

THAT'S WHAT FRIENDS ARE FOR

The day I met Cher my life changed forever. It was in the spring, in art class, when we discovered we were both huge Backstreet Boys fans. Our conversations grew from that, and soon we realized we had a lot in common: We were both figure-skating fanatics, we both loved pasta, and we both shared a passion for Walt Disney movies.

It wasn't long before we were ultimate best friends, doing things that best friends do: eating lunch together, having sleep-overs, going to the movies after school, sharing secrets. She complained to me when her crush didn't smile at her in drama, and I complained about the load of homework my teachers were piling on me.

Trust . . . that seemed to be the key to our friendship. I trusted her with everything, as she did with me.

We seemed to have such a perfect friendship that I began to forget about my other friends. It was just Steph and Cher—best friends forever.

I remember the day it all changed . . . the day she betrayed and hurt me . . . the day she taught me one of the most important lessons of my entire life.

The bus rides to school were always tense—arguments broke out all the time, and insults shot from seat to seat like bolts of lightning.

One Tuesday morning, a girl and I got into a little argument over something so silly that I can't even remember what it was.

Once at school, Cher (being the best friend that she was) told me how much better I was than this other girl, and how much compassion I had for others.

"Write down all the things you don't like about her," she told me in biology class. "It will make you feel better."

Looking back at it now, I realize how naive and immature I was to do so. But I was feeling grumpy, and I didnt want it to ruin my day. Wanting to be free of those feelings, I wrote the list and Cher and I giggled about it for the rest of the period. After all, it was a secret shared between two best friends . . . or so I thought.

The next day, Cher wasn't at the bus stop, and I soon found out why. She had shown the list to the other girl, who was furious. The girl wrote her own list about me, which she read in front of the entire bus. But that wasn't what hurt me, what caused me to choke back tears. It was the fact that my best friend, the person I trusted most in the entire school, had turned around and back-stabbed me.

She had tricked me, and then phoned me that night as if nothing had happened. Still hurt and angry, I told her she had a lot of nerve to call me, and demanded to know what she wanted.

At first, she denied ever showing her the list, but fell silent when I asked, "How come the girl was holding my list in her hand?"

"She got it out of my school bag" was Cher's next excuse.

I ended the conversation by telling her that our friendship was over, and hung up. Perhaps not the most mature thing to do, but I was enraged that she couldn't even admit her mistake.

I suddenly felt very alone . . . how would I survive being a teenager without my best friend? Then I reminded myself that a true best friend would have never betrayed me.

At school the next day, the friends I had once ditched to be with Cher wrote me little notes telling me that I deserved the best, and how special I was to them. I held each note close to my heart, but my friend Rhoda's was perhaps the most heartwarming:

> Dear Steph,
> Don't worry about it, you've got lots of friends who can help you get through it and who love you. What you should do is make a new list . . . a list about all the things you like about yourself.
> That's the kind of list that will make you feel better. Here, I'll help you get started . . .
>
> > Stephanie is—
> > nice
> > talented
> > fun
> > happy

I smiled at the list and picked up my pen. Without hesitation, the very next "quality" I added to my list was:

> lucky to have Rhoda as a friend.

Cher may have hurt me deeply, but she made me realize something. My *real* friends came to comfort me even though I hadn't eaten lunch with them in over a month. They made it their mission to make me smile, even though I hadn't updated them on my latest crush, or told them what had been bothering me in English. They were just there for me . . . because that's what friends are for.

They took me right back into their circle of endless friendship with loving arms, and never held it against me that I had once abandoned them.

Instead, as we sat laughing and giggling in the cafeteria, my friend Sarah whispered, so softly I could barely hear her, "We missed you, ya know."

And I whispered back, "Same here."

STEPHANIE BERNIER

LOOKING FOR
FAMILIAR CLUES

*T*he sun shone brightly on my dark porcelain skin
as I peeped around the corner observing the big yellow
Ford station wagon pulling in our driveway. The dust
finally settled from the dirt road, and out stepped a tall slender
black man. He wore nothing expensive, nor did he carry a briefcase like the insurance man who often visited my parents on Saturday mornings. He was as observant as I was, and with a glance
caught me looking at him.

I heard him greet my father, who invited him to come in. I was
sixteen then and anxious to know everything. My heart raced
with excitement while I tried to guess why my parents were meeting with this man.

About thirty minutes later, I observed the three of them crowd
the front porch, shaking hands, and watched as the visitor made
his way down the steps. When he looked up, he looked right at
me. Much to my surprise, this time he smiled and winked.

"Alice!" I heard my mother calling. I ran to the front porch, hoping that the riddle in my mind would be answered.

"Come in the house," she said, looking concerned.

John and Sally were the only parents I had ever known. Just a
few weeks before, they had delivered the shocking news that I was
adopted. I could only wonder what my parents were about to re-
veal to me now.

They told me I had a sibling—a brother, who was adopted and
living in Eastside, Tennessee, a town nearby. I decided not to tell

anyone, not even Teresa, my best friend of six years. My brother's adoptive parents had changed his name and when the visitor wanted to give it to me, Sally put her foot down.

This left me determined to find my long-lost brother. I yearned for a part of me that I hadn't even known existed. In my quiet moments, I began wondering: What was my brother like? Did he look like me? And as I thought about him, suddenly and unexpectedly I began grieving for all we had missed.

That's why I said yes to Teresa's invitation to go to Eastside for their back-to-school dance at the armory. Just a month after finding out that I had a brother, I was on my way to his hometown. A smile swept across my face as I sat in the passenger seat of her Mustang.

"What are you smiling about, girl?" Teresa shouted, breaking my train of thought.

"Nothing special, just looking forward to having a good time."

"Well, a good time we are going to have, so hold on because we are on our way to the city of boys, boys, and boys."

"That's what you are going for? I don't need a boyfriend."

"Everyone needs a boyfriend, Alice. And you ain't no different."

"*Aren't any different* is the correct phrase, and I *am* different."

"Whatever, but you got to loosen up tonight, or I am going to drop you off at the next bus stop."

I knew Teresa was teasing, but she was right.

In the armory, the music was loud and couples danced close. The phrase *loosen up* crossed my mind, and I became frightened. This type of dance was different from what I was used to. The lights above changed and started flashing red, green, and yellow dots all over my T-shirt. Disappearing seemed the best solution to everything, but as I hung in there for Teresa, I reminded myself that I'd come here to look for my brother, and that's what I did. I danced with every guy who offered, looking at him for any resemblance to me. Until finally I just had to rest and found an empty chair.

"Your friend can really dance," the boy seated on my left said before he asked me to dance. To my relief, we decided to catch a dance later. Once he left, I realized I hadn't caught his name. He was cute all right, but oh well, he was shorter than me anyway.

The song had ended and Teresa immediately plopped down in the seat beside me.

"Here we go again," Teresa retorted after hearing my reasoning. "If it ain't color, it's height. Girl, you too choosy for me."

"One day you will understand," I replied more softly than she expected.

We left the dance that night, Teresa loaded down with phone numbers. My journey, on the other hand, had ended unsuccessfully. My last dance was with the fellow on my left—the seat-warmer—whom I did not care to get a number from.

I did get one number, though, for my stepbrother Perry. It seems this girl named Kim was still interested in him. So I became the go-between.

Perry didn't seem interested at first, but in the course of conversation, he told me that Kim was from Eastside. Kim's number stayed on my mind for days. I finally called her myself. I don't know why, but I felt compelled to tell her my story—even though I hadn't told my best friend.

Soon Kim and I made a deal. I'd put in a good word to Perry, and she'd ask around about my brother, whose adoption had been secret, and whose name I didn't know. A long shot for sure. At that point, I felt that I had done all I could do. I hadn't given up, but I left the search for my brother up to God.

On a cool October night, Kim came over and stood on the porch with a smile that could replace the sun. *She must be here to see Perry,* I thought, since he had finally gone out with her again.

"I'm not here to see Perry, I'm here to see you," Kim said, reading my mind.

"What about? I kept my promise."

"I know," she answered, "and I want to keep mine." With those few words, she reached behind herself and pulled to her side a young man around my age. His eyes were deep and dark—just like mine. And his skin was also the color of dark porcelain.

"Alice, this is your brother, Willie," Kim said forcing us to meet face to face and for me to see a part of me that I'd been looking for all along.

"You?" he said after pausing, and frowning, and then smiling broadly.

"You?" I said, looking back at him as he mirrored my emotions. Tears filled our eyes, but we both choked back what we were feeling. The flashing lights that night at the armory had blocked my view. Besides, I had assumed the height I carried would be passed on. Definitely the last dance was the best one that night.

At first, we both grieved the loss of years we could have played, laughed, teased, and even comforted each other through the ups and downs. But today, whenever I hear his voice on the telephone, I grin, grateful that a new dance can begin.

ALICE T. CHEEK

STICKS AND STONES

I *grew up in a town with fast cars, fast boys, and lots*
of slow, slow girls. The small but sprouting suburb on Long
Island was a haven for those wanting to raise families outside of the city. The fast boys were the spoiled, wild offspring of
doctors, lawyers, and businesspeople whose success blinded them
from really seeing their children.

I was one of the slow girls, a surrogate sister to the fast boys.
Although I was only fifteen and most of them were eighteen, I
possessed a kind of magical power over them. They seemed fascinated by my innocence, and since some had dropped out of high
school just to hang out, I served as a link to the youth slipping
rapidly from their grasp. They wore their parents' wealth in the
cars they drove—flashy red Corvettes and sleek MGs with real
leather interior. Cars became their limbs; without them they were
powerless and vulnerable.

There was Peter, nicknamed "Butter" because his father owned
bakeries that supplied the public schools. He was tall and blonde
with full ruddy cheeks. Like the Pied Piper, he'd dole out cookies
to neighborhood kids. He smelled of chocolate, which made him
very appealing. Richie was the handsomest and the only son of a
surgeon. He had deep-set hazel eyes that made it hard for me to
catch my breath. He was referred to as "Brain." Everyone expected Richie to take after his father, but there were few signs of
that happening. He was great under the hood of a car, but I
doubted he'd ever make it to the operating room. Jeff, "The Fox,"

was the son of a trial lawyer, a fast talker who made up for being short with his keen sense of humor.

While other boys spent summers working as lifeguards and saving for college, the fast boys were busy cruising up and down the tree-lined streets of our neighborhood, blasting their car radios. They became fixtures in our town, like the tarnished statues posed on the library lawn. The boys were unshaven, unassuming, and unashamed. I'd hear them yelling out their car windows to my friends and me as we walked home from intramurals. They'd howl and laugh in their own secret language. My parents had warned me to keep my distance. Didn't they know that's what made me curious and the boys so appealing?

When I walked home alone, I'd hear their car motors revving up, trailing behind me. "Stickee," they bellowed—this, an abbreviated version of "The Stick," with which they had crowned me. It was a tribute to my skinny and shapeless legs. As they pulled alongside me, they motioned for me to hop on in. My heart kicked, but I took the chance and slipped in quietly while they purred my nickname softly in my ear. "Stickeeeeee."

A strange, peppery smell permeated the air and hurt my eyes. As nervous as I was, I felt safe. They would never hurt me. Brain surveyed my books and notes, checking out all he'd missed. Butter looked through the pictures in my wallet. He liked the little sayings I'd glued over the faces of friends and families. Fox checked out my clothes and gave me tips on getting guys to like me. I thought that it was clear that I didn't need any boyfriends as long as I had them.

By the end of the summer, I'd gained a few pounds. *Filled out,* as my mother liked to say. I was glad to be off those after-school malteds that she forced me to drink. Butter, Brian, and Fox stopped calling me Stickee.

One sizzling humid night, Brain called, asking me to come over to his house for a pool party. It was still light out, and I told my parents that I was going over to a girlfriend's. But when I knocked on the door to Richie's cabana, he appeared sweaty and strange-looking. Music blasted in the background. I walked in and froze, seeing no other guests. I was frightened but tried not to show it. He smelled sour from liquor and he could hardly stand. My hair was up in a French twist and Richie pulled the hairpins out one by one, fluffing my hair with his fingers. In his drunken stupor, he was incapable of doing much more. I winced when he tried to kiss me, and he looked as though he might cry. He passed out and I walked home alone in the dark. The chilly night air reminded me that school would soon begin; this season was sure to end.

I saw the boys less and less. When I did, they appeared tired and restless. They played cards during the day and hung out at the racetrack at night. After school I'd stop at Joe's luncheonette, where they'd be hanging over a racing sheet, going over the picks for the night. One afternoon, I heard them arguing as they slammed in and out of the phone booth. Butter didn't look like Butter. He paced up and down, a cigarette stuck to his bottom lip. There was whispering. I heard them mention some guy named Fats, whom they owed over three Gs. If they didn't come up with "the stash" they'd be "taken out"!

I went home terrified for the boys and furious, too, that they let things go this dangerously far. Their actions had caught up with them, and I realized I was no different. It was time to come clean. I told my parents everything—I'd been living a double life . . . I was a liar. They'd deal with that later, but now my father had to make an important phone call.

The next morning, while I dressed for school, three cars screeched into my driveway. The boys screamed, "*Stickee* get outside!" I stood against the garage door while they berated me for telling about their debt and having a very big mouth.

"Leave her alone," Butter yelled, and I stopped shivering.

"I didn't want any of you to get taken out," I said, before I slumped to the grass crying.

Butter was the first to forgive me. At the end of the year, he signed my yearbook. He started to write Stickee, then crossed it out: "To Sande: a tree will only grow moss if a rambling brook runs alongside." I hoped I was his rambling brook—that in some small way, I might have saved them. Sometimes I'll drive the roads we used to drive—the fast boys and me—although the road seems so much narrower.

SANDE BORITZ BERGER

FROM NOT TO HOT

Why couldn't I be one of them, one of the lucky few that high school's aura of success seemed to touch? As I walked through the halls, I felt a bit invisible, as if I were the background music to someone else's hit song. But today at the fairgrounds, something different was happening. What was it? Maybe it was the open air rather than the confining hallways. Or the cool fall breeze that set me dreaming. All I know is that as I listened to the country music group Atlanta, some new kind of music stirred within me and took hold.

As the group's music filled the air, suddenly it hit me. I could interview this group. Here was my chance to prove I was serious about being a journalist. Feeling buoyant yet businesslike, I approached the manager, a big, king-sized version of Charlie Daniels. With the self-assurance of a seventeen-year-old who didn't realize what she was doing, I set all invisibility aside and asked for the interview.

"Sure, why not?" the man answered before I had a chance to think twice. "How 'bout after their nine o'clock show?"

Errrchhh! My mind started putting on the brakes. What would my parents say? After all, I had school the next day. "Sure," I said without blinking. "Thanks." Then I turned, rushing to my parents to plead my case.

With my dream in hand, I begged my parents to stay late just this once so I could "get my big break." Was this me talking—the person who'd felt second place for so long? Something had definitely changed!

Before I knew it, I was walking toward my dream—and the interview with Atlanta. I was armed with only a ballpoint pen and a single piece of paper—a borrowed one at that.

As I sat down with the two members of the group who'd agreed to speak with me, I hardly knew what to say, or what to ask. My bravado nearly failed me, as it became more and more obvious that I'd never done an interview before and that I knew absolutely nothing about this band!

As I stumbled and I stammered, I noticed something beautiful. They graciously gave me answers to questions that I was too ignorant to ask. My heart welled up in response, as I accepted their kind generosity.

After school the next day, I persuaded my grandmother to take me to the offices of the *Washington County News,* a weekly local paper. To my extreme delight, the editor agreed to run it in the following week's edition. Trying to contain myself, I took another shot. Surely this man could benefit from my writing talent, so I offered to cover the gubernatorial debates later in the week.

"Thank you," he said, "but I already have someone on that." To his credit, I'm sure that he drew in his cheeks and held in his laughter until I'd left the office.

I knew I didn't run with the "in" crowd. I didn't participate in sports, and I was out after the first round of the beauty pageant. My brother seemed to possess the monopoly on the trophies and accomplishment in our family. That is, until Thursday, when I opened up the paper and saw my byline and article under a photograph of the group Atlanta. There it was—my article. It was edited, but it had my name on it and a number of the sentences were mine alone.

I raced to the kitchen, cut out the article, and placed it in an 11-by-14-inch frame. After showing it to every member of the family, including my extended family, I hung it on my bedroom wall.

When I went to school Friday morning, I held my head a little higher and walked with more spring in my step. I walked into English class and stopped midstride—for right in front of me, taped to Mrs. Edmonson's podium, was my article *and* a huge sign that read, CONGRATULATIONS, GAYLE! Blushing, I smiled and hurried to my seat, but on the inside, I was doing the "Snoopy Dance!" Finally, I'd made the winning field goal, batted a home run, won the race, and gotten the highest grade in the class.

As I thought about it, I realized I'd not only tapped into my passion and found some valuable bravado and even courage, but I'd had some help.

On the way home from school, I quietly counted my helpers. From the big-hearted manager, to the kind members of Atlanta, to my parents who bent the rules, to my grandmother who eased my travels, to the editor who didn't laugh at me, to Mrs. Edmonson's celebration. Inside me, I knew this was more than luck.

How could I say thank you? I wondered. Then I imagined all these people smiling, if only I followed my passions and my joy. As I stepped off the bus that day, I felt deeply changed by people who befriended dreams. And I knew that within my byline, there was and would always be a generous gift of grace.

GAYLE TRENT

VIII
PROUD MAMAS

A mother is never cocky or proud,
because she knows the school principal may call at any minute
to report that her child has just driven a motorcycle
through the gymnasium.

MARY KAY BLAKELY

It's when we're given choice
that we sit with the gods and design ourselves.
DOROTHY GILMAN

KELLY'S CHOICE

When my daughter daydreamed about what it would be like in high school, she never imagined being the target of someone's vicious anger, or that the ripples of hatred would be spread by one senior girl to her large circle of friends.

All the joy and the anticipation of entering high school had been torn apart on a summer night in August when Kelly had let another girl's boyfriend steal a kiss from her. She felt terrible about that, and wished she could apologize to Chantelle, the girl-friend. I told her that it would all blow over in time, but I was wrong. The glaring stares and snide whispers from the girl and her friends continued through fall's brilliant color, the arrival of winter's snow, and now into the springtime. Sometimes anger is nurtured into an obsession. Like an addict, it seemed Chantelle was plunging a needle of hatred into her veins each morning.

Finally one spring day in the cafeteria came the confrontation Kelly had dreaded, when the anger boiled over and Chantelle was suddenly in Kelly's face yelling, "I'm going to beat you up today! You better be ready!" In a flash she was gone again, leaving Kelly to walk through the hallways in a daze of anxiety, to sit through classes hearing only the fear throbbing inside of her. She didn't want to report it to the principal's office; she didn't want to be labeled a coward and a tattletale. She didn't know what to do except to face this alone.

Suddenly, near the end of the school day when Kelly was walking down the hallway, there she was in the open courtyard inside the school.

"I'm going to beat you up for what you did!" Chantelle screamed at her.

A crowd quickly gathered, and soon there were a couple of hundred students encircling them—so many that even teachers couldn't make it through the throng.

Kelly put her hands out. "Chantelle, I'm sorry. This is stupid—we can talk this out." Kelly pleaded and tried to reason with the bigger girl, but her words bounced off an immovable object.

Chantelle suddenly lunged and viciously pulled Kelly's hair, began beating her with open hands, and grabbed and ripped her shirt halfway off. Kelly was stunned and shaken, and all she could think of was to stop her attacker. In a split second she did what her father had taught her to do if she ever had to defend herself. She closed her fist, pulled her elbow back, and then sent a straight shot to Chantelle's nose and watched as the senior girl crumpled to the ground and blood splashed around her.

It was over. And yet it was far from over. Kelly and Chantelle were both immediately suspended from school for five days, according to their high school's policy of zero tolerance for violence. After a plea from me that my daughter was just defending herself, the superintendent did reduce Kelly's suspension. However, it was small consolation to Kelly, and the fact that from then on Chantelle and her friends avoided her like the plague didn't really help her feel that much better either.

She was only a freshman, and the administrators had already labeled her a troublemaker in her school. From now on, they would be watching her every move and her reputation would follow her everywhere. It was disheartening and depressing to think that everyone knew who she was because of the trouble she'd been in. I knew how bad my daughter felt about being suspended for fighting, for missing her volleyball games during that time, for feeling that she'd let her team down, herself down.

"Kelly, honey, when you graduate with honors, I'm going to frame that suspension form and hang it on the wall," I said while hugging her tightly.

And after that, it became Kelly's goal not to let one negative situation brand and define who she was. She became determined to succeed, and to wipe out her label as a troublemaker.

And succeed she did.

Today, if you were to visit our home, you would see a suspension form matted and framed and hung on the living room wall. It hangs next to Kelly's Most Valuable Player awards, her Team Captain honors, her Best Athlete and Best Scholar-Athlete plaques, her Good Citizenship and High Honors certificates, and a photograph of Kelly as homecoming queen.

Kelly's spirit and accomplishments have all but erased the stereotype that began her high school years. The turmoil and negative reputation that once followed her through the school hallways is all but forgotten now, and all that remains of that darker time is a small piece of paper hanging on a wall.

ANNE GOODRICH

THE ONE-YEAR RULE

P *arents who impose strict rules on their teenagers* have a better chance of raising drug-free children, according to a study by the National Center on Addiction and Substance Abuse, based at Columbia University. Why am I not surprised? Since I've been slipping and sliding with my daughters on this rocky road of adolescence for more than a dozen years, I've created a rule or two of my own. As if it were a much-worn flannel bathrobe, I am not ready to part with my favorite rule: the one-year rule.

It was a good ten years ago over a relaxed Sunday dinner of pasta and salad when my preadolescent daughter bemoaned yet again the fact that she had no life. "I have no life" in adolescent speak translates to "I have no boyfriend." As I ladled out the spaghetti sauce, I announced to my three blue-eyed daughters that I had formulated a new family rule: They were not allowed to date anyone who was more than a year older than they were. Since the oldest, Abby, was barely twelve, Susie was ten, and Vicky was a five-year-old dragging her beat-up blankey everywhere, they stared at one another in disbelief. My husband shrugged his shoulders, Abby smirked, Susie rolled her eyes, and Vicky sucked her thumb.

"So this means Vicky can't go out with a second-grader?" the older two asked, smiling at the absurdity. But I played along, insisting a smooth-talking seven-year-old was out of the question. I knew that jumping in with rules, stating values, and taking positions before the child is issue-ready makes sense, a bit like the marines and military preparedness.

How and why did I come up with this arbitrary piece of family legislation, my daughters have since asked me. A rule that actually limited the boyfriend playing field. I can clearly trace the one-year rule's beginnings to the summer I was thirteen, when my mother died. My father listened to downbeat Frank Sinatra songs and sipped whiskey. My brothers and I did whatever we wanted. Discipline with my parents had always been slack, but now it was nonexistent. I had no curfew, never had to call home. I could run wild. This freedom should have been a prescription for a teenager's delight, but I felt curiously unsafe and afraid of risk.

Back then, on muggy July nights, my best friend, Kathy, and I would walk a half mile or so to the corner drugstore, order a soda at the counter, and wait for boys to come in. Kathy, a cute, freckled-faced cheerleader, was a sophisticated fifteen, already a high-school junior. She knew more than I did. She knew when my mother was pregnant and I did not. I would pretend I got her jokes and mentally file words away to look up in the dictionary later.

One quiet Friday night, Richie and Gordie, dark, curly-haired cousins, strutted into the drugstore for cigarettes. Richie was seventeen, movie-star handsome in a hair-gel kind of way, and interested in Kathy. Gordie was sixteen, thin, and a talker; mine by default. I could tell Gordie liked me, though, by how close he stood to me, how he paid attention to my every word. After three or four meetings of hanging out on the street corner, Gordie and Richie decided to up the social ante.

Gordie, ever the spokesman, suggested that we go for a walk in the park. The isolated neighborhood park. I can still feel the chill of goosebumps on my upper arms. I could see the outline of the pack of cigarettes in the rolled-up sleeve of Gordie's T-shirt, the perfectly sculptured curl in the middle of his forehead. Kathy wanted to go and begged me to say yes. Gordie and Richie prodded. It was just a walk in the park. What was I afraid of? they demanded. In that early evening dusk, sensing danger, the seeds of a lifelong hypervigilance sprouted in me. I said no to Gordie. Kathy said nothing, shot me a look of disgust, and walked off with Gordie and Richie. I walked home alone.

The friendship faded after that night as if it had been washed with the wrong laundry detergent. No, I did not pluck the one-year rule out of the empty air. I would be the parent I didn't have.

Abby and Susie are young women now; only Vicky, at fifteen, is still a teenager. By now, I've watched boyfriends come and go, but the one-year rule still stands. Perhaps it was a liking for the simple math, or the absence of boys in their young lives, but my daughters accepted and embraced the one-year rule that night at the dinner table. While I want to empower my daughters' choices, I also want to hand them the safety of that time-honored excuse: "My parents would kill me."

The one-year rule has been bandied about by my daughters in college dorms and sororities, mocked, discussed with friends, and better yet, adopted by other parents. I feel a distinct pride of ownership. I have conceded that at some point the one-year rule, like the time-out chair, will fade into oblivion, but as far as I know it hasn't happened yet. Not on my watch.

CAROLE GAUNT

WHEN
YES MEANS NO

*E*veryone knows that good communication is key to happy relationships between teens and adults. But sometimes the rules we set up can be distorted by nature's twisted sense of humor.

Several years ago, when my son Nathan had just barely crossed the threshold into his teenage years, our family was invited to spend the day water-skiing with friends who'd just purchased a brand-new boat. Their thirteen-year-old daughter and her best friend came along. It was a beautiful hot summer day, and we were all looking forward to dipping our toes in the lake.

I packed a picnic lunch and the video camera hoping to capture on tape our family having fun on film. Lately, Nathan's surging hormones had erased all his happy childhood memories and replaced them with fully restored images of every parental mistake I'd ever made.

Since none of us had ever water-skied before, we decided to start slow and send Nathan out first on a Boogie Board—figuring he was young and would heal faster. Wary at first, he eventually complied when I convinced him that we were adults and would stop the boat the minute he got scared, cold, or dismembered.

I consider myself quite the communicator, and therefore decided to establish the rules for communication from Boogie Board to boat. I instructed Nathan to use a series of head movements, since he would need to keep both hands on the Boogie Board handle. Nod up and down for "go faster," and side to side for "slow down." Easy enough.

He jumped in the water and with very little effort got centered perfectly on the board and indicated he was ready to give it a try.

The captain accelerated slowly, and we all watched in amazement as our neophyte aquanaut began to rise up and out of the water like Neptune Jr.

"By God, he's a natural!" I yelled, and my husband started the video rolling to record what appeared to be the first signs of something I hadn't seen Nathan do in months. Smile. He was having a good time with his parents, and darn it, I wanted proof for posterity's sake.

Gradually the boat sped up enough to give a smooth steady ride and shortly thereafter we saw Nathan's head nodding up and down to go faster. We obeyed his order. Surprisingly, a few minutes later he was nodding again, only this time with a look of fierce determination. Although I was surprised by his need for speed, I signaled the captain to take it up a notch. The girls were definitely impressed.

These are the moments that parents live for. Watching our teenage children exceed our expectations. And even though I couldn't hear what he was saying at the end of that rope, I knew we were communicating one on one. Even my husband complimented me on the head signal system and asked if I'd use it with him at home instead of talking as much as I do.

Nathan remained amazingly steady on the Boogie Board in spite of the fact that the boat's wake was creating a bit of chop on the water's surface. The sunlight glistened on his gangly frame, his hair flapping in the wind like a dog's ears hanging out the car window. It was beautiful. I smiled and waved to him and he nodded vigorously to go faster.

Now, at this point, I wasn't sure that was a good idea. We were already going fast enough for the seat cushions to flutter, but my husband agreed that Nathan was indeed nodding for more, and so we acquiesced.

After we'd circled the lake at least twelve more times I wondered how long our young dynamo could last. And then I saw the unbelievable. His head began nodding again. No, I said, we've created a monster, a glutton for punishment . . . a speed freak! The captain agreed, and as responsible adults we decided to end Nathan's Boogie Board madness and bring the boat to a stop.

I could hear him yelling long before the motor cut off. Being a teenager, he wouldn't understand that this was one of those parental decisions that had to be made for his own good. I was prepared to defend my position.

"Are you trying to kill me?" He was screaming in a fury peppered with expletives that I still can't find definitions for. "Why'd you keep going faster?!"

I was totally confused. Up and down meant faster, side to side meant slower. That was what we'd agreed upon, no?

"I wasn't nodding! My head was bobbing up and down from the waves and I couldn't stop it 'cause you kept going faster and faster!" he explained.

And all of this on video, of course. It was hard to tell whom the girls were laughing at more, me or Nathan.

Suddenly my finely honed communication skills were reduced to a series of inaudible grunts and sputters as I groveled for forgiveness. I asked Nathan what I could do to make it up to him, and he came back with a rather effective suggestion. He said I should watch the video once a year on my birthday. That way I'd be reminded that real communication involves more than just one person's perspective. The girls inched toward Nathan nodding their heads up and down in agreement.

Who says teens can't communicate? Maybe we just don't know how to listen.

Now, if you'll excuse me, it's my birthday and I have a video I've been instructed to watch.

CAROL F. FANTELLI

A CLASS ACT

*O*n a spring day eleven years ago, riding home from nursery school, my daughter, Sylvia, spied three or four toddlers in pastel leotards with stiff, short skirts of matching net. They were spinning like tops, arms straight out from their sides, tiny, pink-slippered toes stepping in close circles. "I want to do that!" she announced. "Mom, look! I want to do that!"

The first day at dance school, Sylvia made a less-than-graceful entrance, cowering in the folds of my skirt.

"It's okay," the teacher said, smiling, and the leathery creases at the corners of her bright blue eyes deepened. "They're often shy at first. Keep bringing her. She'll begin to enjoy herself."

Each Tuesday afternoon, we returned to the bright white studio in the local high-school annex with the tall windows looking out on a grove of swaying eucalyptus that seemed to keep time with the waltzes and mazurkas emanating from the boom box in the corner of the sun-filled room.

The teacher was right. Sylvia began to enjoy herself. The students danced roles from favorite fairy tales. They twirled, pointed toes, and leapt from imaginary stage right to stage left and back again. At the end of class, they sat in a circle, pointing and flexing, pointing and flexing. For the finale, they stood and the teacher led them through a closing bow. "P for passé, plié coupe." The teacher leaned forward and took each pair of hands, folded one long leg gracefully behind the other, and nodded a farewell to each little dancer.

Eventually, the chubby preschoolers slimmed. Thin legs extended from beneath gauzy nylon skirts. Shoulders, chins, elbows revealed themselves in poses sustained to present form and grace and style. Formerly unruly knots of hair clutched in bits of brightly colored elastic were smoothed into the ubiquitous bun at the crown of the head. There was no more exuberant twirling at the top of the concrete steps outside the doors of the school.

Real dancers now, they stood in extreme self-consciousness, silently awaiting the casting sheets for the upcoming holiday performances. Big eyes took in the names written next to boldfaced roles. Clenched muscles along fragile jaw lines were the only signs of reaction. Most read wordlessly and walked away. Outside, some wept alone. Others hugged, splashing tears on bared shoulders. Euphoria and disappointment stood side by side in gauze and spandex and netting.

Each year, the casting was inexplicable. A child with insolent eyes and a serious gum-chewing habit was a featured demisoloist who fell from her pointe shoes with a clownish grin and a casual shrug. A tiny, charismatic girl with silvery blonde hair was hidden in the last row of a large corps piece where she danced unseen and flawlessly. It was rumored that children with mothers who sewed satin bodices and tulle tutus got the best parts.

If it was corrupt, it was also remarkable. There were no auditions. It was even free to those who could not pay. The sole requirement for the opportunity to perform was a love of dance and a commitment to attend rehearsals. The curtains rose on an expansive vinyl floor placed, strip by strip, by parent volunteers. The opening andante movement of Tchaikovsky's score was released into the air. An audience of parents, brothers, sisters, grandparents, teachers, and friends awaited each dancer's entrance, erupting in proud applause at the end of each scene, each variation, and the finale, during which each cast member came forward and bowed over a heart beating in double time.

It went on like that for eleven years until Sylvia's best friend and two others were cast in the lead roles. As the best friend was hugged and congratulated outside, my daughter, silent and dismayed, was led into the glass-walled office by the teacher, who said, "If you weren't so tall, you would be my lead dancer." Adolescence had intervened, but failed to dampen the love of the pirouette, rond de jambe, and pas de deux. The teacher was generous, rewarding her enthusiasm, determination, and skill with many parts, all of which were highly visible by the audience.

At rehearsals, I watched one of the lead dancers stumble repeatedly and tangle her satin-covered feet in the sash of her costume; another had missed many rehearsals and remained uncertain of the choreography. I watched my daughter, who, having learned her own parts, volunteered to help those dancers uncertain of their steps; I watched her spend her free time playing with restless younger dancers during long rehearsals.

"Why?" I asked angrily and loudly of myself and any other willing listener. "Why does she spend all of her time at that dance school, accepting the pronouncement that what she is isn't good enough? Why doesn't Sylvia swim competitively, measuring herself against an objective stopwatch instead of allowing herself to be measured by a subjective art form that says participants must be this size and that size, depending upon gender and role? Why isn't she slam-dunking her way through high school? Why? Why? Why?

Two days before opening night, I walked into the house and saw Sylvia's black Capezio bag and toeshoes in a heap at the bottom of the stairs. A hamstring, torn at rehearsal, would not heal for six weeks. Her father and I had been driving to rehearsals four times a week for three months and would not see any of her hard work put together with music and costume on stage. I felt something approaching guilty relief.

Three hours before the first show I was groping in the darkness of a foul, holiday-infested mood, trying to think of something we could do to take our minds off of what was going to happen on-stage, without us. Sylvia came into my room.

"Mom, I need to shop for presents for my friends and take them to the theater before the show starts. Maria is filling in for me in the first-act solo. Can we get her some flowers? And Jennifer, Sierra, and Camille gave me a surprise birthday party at the studio. They even made a cake. Can I get them something?"

Downtown, I followed a few paces behind as she maneuvered crutches across a cracked and narrow sidewalk.

Two hours later, I pulled up to the theater. "I'll park the car and bring these gifts in."

"No, thanks," Sylvia said, reaching behind the seat for the shopping bag filled with boxes and flowers, "I can manage. They'll need my help backstage. Could you pick me up after the show?"

I watched her grow smaller and smaller and finally disappear behind the stage door.

That night, her father and I met her outside the silent emptied theatre with a bouquet of pink roses. "Bravo," we whispered, with tremors, hugging each other in the dark.

NANCY SMITH HARRIS

It's always been my feeling that God lends you your children
until they're about eighteen years old.
If you haven't made your points with them by then, it's too late.
BETTY FORD

SAY WHAT?

O ne night, as my twelve-year-old daughter and I
were watching a television show, the show's host
asked a teenage girl how the teen's mother had most
influenced her life. The girl proceeded to rave about her remarkable mother and the important life lessons she had passed on
to her. This teenager had all but built a shrine in honor of her
mother.

My mind began to wander and I pondered what my own
daughter would say about me if asked this same question. Most of
the time it seems we parents have little, if any, idea what impact
we've had on our children.

Hmmm . . . what gems had I passed along to my daughter?
Would she say that I'd taught her to be strong and independent,
outspoken and unconventional? Would she give me *all* the credit
for her successes? Which, of course, is what we needy mothers
are looking for. Take, for example, the movie star who has just
won an Academy Award and, with tears in her eyes and a soulful
expression on her face, she breathlessly announces on worldwide
television, "Mom, I couldn't have done this without you. This is

for you." Yeah, that's what moms want, credit for something other than doing your laundry.

I nudged my daughter and inquired, "Hey, Liza, if you were asked that question, how would you answer it? What would you say is the most important life lesson that I've taught you?"

I didn't have to wait long for her answer. Liza shot from the hip, no hesitation. She rapidly responded, "Don't wear white shoes after Labor Day."

What?

She repeated her response. No equivocation. She gave me an irritated look as if to say, "Didn't you hear me the first time, Mom?"

I had. Loud and clear.

I didn't know whether to laugh or cry. Sometimes, not often, but sometimes, a child knows instinctively when her mother is right and simply accepts what she says. Yet it was still disconcerting to discover that the most crucial tidbit of information I'd passed along to my daughter in the first twelve years of her life was, heaven forbid, Don't wear white shoes after Labor Day.

I guess I won't be mentioned when *she* wins her Oscar. But, by golly, she won't be wearing white shoes after Labor Day either. I can guarantee you that.

CINDI PEARCE

SAVING THE BEST FOR LAST

Growing up, my older brother and I fought a lot about food. For my part, it wasn't that I was hungry; it was just that the only oyster left in the pan, or the last slice of pie, or the remaining piece of candy in the sack seemed more intriguing if I could beat my brother to it.

Every time we launched into a squabble over who got the last bit of a favorite food, Dad would interrupt us and say in a matter-of-fact conversational sort of way, "It tastes better when you share."

We weren't convinced that the prized tidbit would really taste better if we shared it, but hearing him say those words always gave us pause. Especially since Dad always shared everything.

Now I use that same technique with my children, but I've found it sometimes works too well.

For example, recently I settled down in the recliner to savor the last piece of the fresh apple pie my mother had brought over.

I was about to take that first satisfying bite when I heard my teenage daughter, Barbara Jean, ask, "Mom, will you share it?"

"I'd really rather not," I responded in one of my selfish moments.

Dead silence until Barbara Jean said, "It tastes better when you share."

I paused.

"It really doesn't, you know," I replied, hoping that would

work. To which I received only a silent nod of acknowledgment. Reluctantly, I got up to cut the piece of pie in half.

A few days later my mother delivered a small plate of her freshly baked delicacies—still-warm-from-the-oven cinnamon rolls with caramelized sugar frosting drizzled on the top of each one.

They are my daughter's favorite treat.

And there were only four of them.

Barbara Jean walked in the front door after track practice looking very hungry. She spotted the rolls on the kitchen counter and, as quickly as running the one hundred-yard dash, she downed two of them with a frosty glass of milk.

My cinnamon roll went down a little slower as I savored each bite and licked the frosting from my fingers like a cat giving its coat a leisurely grooming.

It wasn't until bedtime that my daughter and I realized we had the same intent when both of us made our way into the kitchen at the same time to pour ourselves another glass of milk and grab that last lonely roll. Her star track record paid off. She got to the finish line first, and the tasty, sticky treat rested in the palm of her hand.

Hmmmm, I mused. Wasn't this the same teenager who only last week managed to work the family's "It tastes better when you share" proverb to get half of my slice of apple pie?

Knowing how quickly she managed to devour the first two cinnamon rolls, I thought it best not to waste time.

"It tastes better when you share, you know," I said.

Her mouth stayed open in midflight, ready to bite into her favorite food. For a moment, both the roll and open mouth stood frozen in time.

"You know, Grandpa was just kidding when he said that," she reasoned, to which I gave a silent nod of acknowledgment.

After a long pause, her reluctant voice yielded to tradition and conscience. "Hand me a knife," she said.

We each savored our bedtime snack: a glass of cold milk and half of a cinnamon roll.

When we finished eating, we looked at each other and smiled, realizing that "sharing" is a tradition too sweet to let go of.

BARBARA ANN DUSH

MORE CHOCOLATE STORIES?

Do you have a short story you want published that fits the essence of *Chocolate for a Teen's Spirit* or *Chocolate for a Teen's Soul*? I am planning future editions, using a similar format, that will feature love stories, divine moments, overcoming obstacles, following our intuition, or embarrassing moments and humorous stories that teach us to laugh at ourselves. I am seeking touching stories of one to four pages in length that warm our hearts and encourage us to learn and grow.

I invite you to join me in these future projects by sending your special true story for consideration. If your story is selected, you will be paid $100, you'll be listed as a contributing author, and a biographical paragraph about you will be included. For more information, or to send a story, please contact:

Kay Allenbaugh
P. O. Box 2165
Lake Oswego, Oregon 97035

Or visit my Web site, www.chocolateforwomen.com, and read the sample teen stories under "Chocolate Sampler," then e-mail me your story.

kay@allenbaugh.com

CONTRIBUTORS

BETTY AUCHARD is a retired public school art teacher whose textile designs have been published in several periodicals and books. She began writing after her husband died in 1998 and has had numerous short stories and poems accepted for publication. She is an active member of the California Writer's Club. Btauchard@aol.com

SHERRY BENNETT is new on the writing scene. As a native Texan and successful hairstylist, she loves to tell stories from behind the chair. Not until longtime client and friend Kathy Pimentel took her to a creative-writing class did she try putting her stories down on paper and in turn discover her passion for writing. She says, "Writing allows me to view past negative experiences as resources and fodder for adding tension to my plots." Kathy and Sherry are now coauthoring a novel. (408) 529-1646

SANDE BORITZ BERGER began writing as a teenager because her letters amused her parents and "they finally heard me." For several years she got sidetracked in the corporate world writing and producing promotional video programs, until finally returning to her passion. A poet, essayist, and fiction writer, she has written for *Every Woman Has a Story*, published by Warner Books, and for *Cup of Comfort*, published by Adams Media. Her essays are also included in *Ophelia's Mom*, published by Crown, about the trials of raising adolescent daughters. She has completed a novel about a young woman's boredom in 1970s suburbia and its consequences. She lives on Long Island and Manhattan with her "first reader" husband, Steven, and has two extremely independent hardworking daughters. MurphyFace@aol.com

STEPHANIE BERNIER is a fourteen-year-old student living in Quebec. She enjoys creative writing, reading, collecting penguins, singing, shopping, and being with her friends and family. A competitive figure skater trained by Coach Marika Patoto, she dreams of one day competing in the Canadian Nationals. Stephanie dedicates her story with love to her mother, Wendy.

DIANE GONZALES BERTRAND models the creative writing process to her students by writing and publishing her own essays, novels, and poetry. She is the author of *Lessons of the Game, Trino's Choice,* and *Sweet Fifteen,* all published by Arte Publico Press in Houston. She dedicated her new novel, *Trino's Time,* to the history professor who inspired her story in this book. She teaches writing at St. Mary's University in San Antonio. Dbertrand@stmarytx.edu

STEPHANIE RAY BROWN has been happily married to her high-school sweetheart, Terry, for fifteen years. She enjoys sharing stories about raising their two children, six-year-old Savannah and three-year-old Cameron. Their love story can be read in the book *Love Letters of a Lifetime.* savvysdad@aol.com

RENIE SZILAK BURGHARDT was born in Hungary and came to the United States in 1951 as a teenager. She is a freelance writer with many credits in magazines, books, and online publications. Some publications in which her work has appeared are the *Listening to the Animals* series by *Guideposts, Angels on Earth, Cup of Comfort, Whispers from Heaven,* and *God Allows U-Turns 2.* She lives in the country in Doniphan, Missouri, and loves reading, writing, music, and spending time with her family. renieburghardt@semo.net

APRIL BURK says she still gets excited when traveling to other states and countries, and she also enjoys spending time at home in Archer, Florida, with her husband, Samuel P. Clark, and their daughters, Kayla and Sophie. She loves reading, walking, bicycling, movies, and writing. Her stories have appeared in the anthologies *A 5th Portion of Chicken Soup for the Soul; Forks in the Road; Mother Voices;* and *Pandemonium, or Life with Kids* (rereleased as *I Killed June Cleaver*). Her magazine writing includes *Florida Monthly Magazine; ByLine; Florida Living; Hip Mama; Mothering; Parents;* and *Welcome Home.*

ALICE T. CHEEK is a former guest columnist for the *Asheboro Courier Tribune Newspaper,* spends most of her time writing short stories and screenplays, and is aspiring to release her first novel, *Achievements of Color.* A native of Ramseur, North Carolina, she enjoys spending time with her son and serving in her church. The trials that she went through as a child have given her stronger faith and patience as an adult. Her motto is "Every work you do is a self-portrait of yourself. Autograph your work with excellence." (336) 869-1121

MARILYN D. DAVIS is a freelance writer living in the Chicago area. Her short stories and personal essays have been published in the local print media and at various Web sites. Her bachelor's and master's degrees are in education, and she has worked in both teaching and administrative capacities in educational settings ranging from preschool through college. She is married and the mother of two boys, ages ten and fourteen, who provide her an endless source of material for her writings and who make her grateful every day for her sense of humor.

BARBARA ANN DUSH writes nonfiction based on her family experiences growing up in Clarks, Nebraska. Her award-winning newspaper stories have included a focus on prisoner-of-war veterans, a series on Holocaust survivors, and a series on the homeless. Other reports have been on women in World War II, a Vietnam soldier killed in action, and AIDS patients. She is consistently a winner for her feature stories in the annual Nebraska Press Association and Nebraska Press Women contests. She now resides in Fullerton, Nebraska.

CAROL F. FANTELLI was born in Cleveland and received her BAA from Meredith College in 1977 in Raleigh, North Carolina. She began her career as a forensic facial reconstruction artist in 1982 working with various law enforcement agencies, reconstructing the faces of victims for identification purposes. She published her first forensic mystery in 1997, titled *The Face Finder*. She has completed a second forensic mystery in a new series and is working on her third book at present. Carol's books are based loosely on her twenty years of experience as a forensic sculptor and are works of fiction. Facefinders@aol.com

JACQUELYN B. FLETCHER is a freelance writer and editor in Minneapolis. She is currently writing children's books and laughing a lot. JacqueBFletcher@aol.com

JUDITH MORTON FRASER , M.F.T., is a psychotherapist, a writer, and an actress in Los Angeles. Her musical director husband, Ian, is an eleven-time Emmy Award winner; daughter, Tiffany, is an actress; son, Neal, is a chef; and grandchildren Grace, Chelsea, and Jenna are creative works in progress. (323) 656-9800

CAROLE GAUNT is a Broadway producer and an award-winning playwright *(Dance of the Seven-Headed Mouse)*. She is a member of both Mystery Writers of America and Sisters in Crime. Currently she is writing a memoir on her childhood and the early deaths of both her parents. Because of her family background and the events of September 11, 2001, she is working on setting up grief programs in schools dealing with early parental loss. An active board member of the alcoholism Council of New York, she lives in New York City with her husband, David, and is the mother of three daughters.

NANCY B. GIBBS is a pastor's wife, the mother of three grown children, and a grandmother. She is a weekly religion columnist, author, and freelance writer. She is a contributing writer to *Chicken Soup for the Soul, Guideposts Books, Honor Books, Stories for the Heart,* and *Heartwarmers.* She is the author of *Celebrate Life . . . Just for Today* and has also been published in numerous magazines such as *Family Circle, Woman's World, Angels on Earth, Happiness,* and *Decision.* Daiseydood@aol.com

ANNE GOODRICH works as a Webmaster for an educational service agency by day and as creator and Webmaster of OhAngel.com (www.ohangel.com) at night. She lives next to a cornfield in Kalamazoo, Michigan, with her twelve-year-old son, Carman, and one very ill-mannered cat. She loves visits from her two grown children, Gordon and Kelly (but wishes they would take the cat with them when they leave), reading anything she can get her hands on, and occasionally painting a story with words.

NANCY SMITH HARRIS is a native Pennsylvanian whose work has appeared in the *San Francisco Chronicle, The Sun,* and many regional publications in Northern California. She lives in San Rafael with her husband, Peter, daughter, Sylvia, and son, Bob.

BETH BOSWELL JACKS has work that has been accepted for publication in a number of magazines, including *Ladybug, Hopscotch, Shining Star, Kids' Highway, Boys' Quest, Lighthouse Story Collections, Working Writer, The Balanced Woman, Lonzie's Fried Chicken, Devo'zine, Chocolate for a Woman's Dreams, Story Mates, Story Friends,* and *U.S. Kids.* A weekly personal essay columnist for the Cleveland (Mississippi) *Bolivar Commercial,* she has also published one book of creative nonfiction, *Grit, Guts, and Baseball,* a story of sports and race relations in the Mississippi Delta. A full member of the Society of Children's Book Writers and Illustrators, she lives with her husband and basset hound in Cleveland, Mississippi. jaxgbt@tecinfo.com

ALANA JENKINS is a tenth-grader at Wilson High School near Henryetta, Oklahoma. She has been involved in FFA and 4-H for seven years, showing pigs, sheep, rabbits, and chickens. She has participated in Tae Kwon Do for five years, holding the rank of brown belt. She is a member of the Church of Christ, and her hobbies include sewing and reading.

CHERYL JENKINS is a seventeen-year-old high-school senior and attends Wilson High School near Henryetta, Oklahoma. She has served as reporter and vice-president of her FFA chapter, and has shown pigs and sheep for eight years. She has studied martial arts for five years and recently earned her black belt in Tae Kwon Do. She works part-time in her father's veterinary clinic and is a member of the Church of Christ. jjinxdvm@aol.com

JUDITH BADER JONES grew up in a Mississippi River town. She began writing at an early age to make sense of her world. One of her poems was chosen by the "Painters and Poets Project" in Kansas City, "Spotlight Gallery," October 2000. *The Season of Light,* a holiday anthology, published one of her short stories, and she has a poem in *Explorations 2000.* She lives and writes in the Kansas City area. (913) 831-2074. jbjones8@swbell.net

LISA KAUFMAN is a native of Georgia. After following a handsome military man around the world for nearly twenty years she's finally settled in rural northern Alabama. Her busy life is shared with a husband, two sons, and a host of pets. She enjoys life to the fullest by staying close to God, her family, and her heart's passion, writing. Her poetry has appeared in *Portals Poetry Magazine* and she reviews books for *Poetic Voices,* an online poetry magazine. She is an adoptee and cares deeply about the issues surrounding the adoption and reunion process. Whenever possible she lends her time and efforts to this issue. At this time she is working on a collection of short stories and a novel, but never both in the same day! clk@iname.com

KIM KEENAN , MSW, LCSW, has spent fifteen years working with families as a social worker in the field of child welfare and mental health. She is currently working on her high-school teaching certificate in hopes of educating teens in communications and life skills. When not doing laundry, she enjoys writing children's books, short stories, and greeting cards. She recently completed her first novel, *The Diary of Claire,* about a child's journey through family alcoholism. She lives in Peoria, Illinois, along with her husband and two children. (309) 691-0525

WENDY (REID CRISP) LESTINA is a public speaker and the author of two books: *100 Things I'm Not Going to Do Now That I'm Over 50;* and *Do as I Say Not as I Did: Perfect Advice from an Imperfect Mother,* both from Penguin/Putnam/Perigee. She was formerly a magazine editor (*Savvy*) and the national director of the National Association for Female Executives. She has an honorary Doctor of Letters degree from Middlebury College, Middlebury, Vermont.

She lives on a farm in Northern California with her husband, John. annabel144@yahoo.com

BEVERLY C. LUCEY has published fiction in *Portland Maine Magazine*, *Flint River Review*, and *Moxie*, and four of her stories appear in *We Teach Them All*, published by Stenhouse Press. She edits two e-zines: www.languagewrangler.com for educators and word lovers and www.womanofacertainage.com. She can also be seen in e-zines: *TW3 ezine, Zoetrope All-Story Extra—Gift Wrap*, and *Vestal Review—Waiting for the Flight*. She is an instructor of education at Agnes Scott College.

BRIANNA MAHIN-AYERS is eighteen years old and is currently an English major at the University of California at Davis. Some of her favorite nonacademic activities include backpacking, swimming, attending church, and, of course, writing. She is a member of the South Bay Branch of the California Writer's Club, a columnist for a local newsletter, and a frequent contributor to the school newspaper. She has taken a great many pieces of paper to college, as she plans to write her way through the next four years just as she has done every day of her life. bfmahinayers@ucdavis.edu

ROBIN MICHELLE MENDOZA, MS, CCC, is a speech language pathologist and special education teacher in the public schools. She has had her poetry appear in *Womankind, In Friendship's Garden,* and *This Is My Beloved.* She lives with her best friend and husband, Alfredo; two wonderful children, Christian and Brandon; and loyal cat, Rio, in San Carlos, California. She feels so blessed to have the love and support of her family and friends. mllelapin@pacbell.net

CAROL SJOSTROM MILLER lives in New Jersey with her husband, Jack, and daughter, Stephanie. Looking for something quiet to do during her daughter's naps, she started writing and hasn't looked back. Carol's articles and essays have been published in a variety of national and regional magazines, and she is currently pursuing her master's degree in English and publishing at Rosemont College. miller_carol@usa.net

EMILY MOOREHEAD is a published humorist and essayist. She is often referred to as "a piece of work." Humor editor for *eThis! Magazine,* she is a full-time online writer and lives in the wilds of Greater Hermitville, located in rural Tennessee. A frequent contributor to numerous online e-zines, including *Themestream,* she has had work featured in *Headlight Journal, Ennui Magazine,* and *Harry Saratoga.* She earned her Ph.D. from the University of the Streets, majoring in urbanity and wackiness. emlin@multipro.com

LAURIE NUCK is a bilingual elementary teacher who graduated from Boise State University in Idaho. She currently resides in King City, California. She first appeared in the *Chocolate* series with "The Popcorn Can" in *Chocolate for a Lover's Heart.* Her writing, "The Magic of Family Literacy," was published in 1995 in *Portals,* an international reading journal. Her poems include "The Archivist," in *The Mystical Night* anthology, and "The Smile," in *Teen Love on Friendship.* She claims that life is a story waiting to be written and encourages her students to make theirs a success story starting now! bunya@redshift.com

TAMRA B. ORR is a full-time professional writer and author living in northern Indiana. She knows that moments like this with her children are too precious to miss, so she writes from home for many national magazines—stepping over toys and putting in earplugs in order to do so. She writes books on home schooling and nonfiction children's books and has been blissfully married to

Joseph for twenty years. Most important, she is mother to Jasmine, Nicole, Caspian, and Coryn—her inspirations, her challenges, and her blessings. orrbarker@kconline.com

CINDI PEARCE has a bachelor's degree in journalism from Ohio University, and for years has worked as a newspaper reporter/columnist/editor and photographer. She is a freelance writer, and her fiction has appeared nine times in *Star Magazine* and has also appeared in *True Love, True Romance,* and *True Experience* magazines. She has worked as a contract writer for a teen-pregnancy prevention project and Family and Children First Council. She has also worked as a court advocate for a domestic violence agency; a choreographer; a tap dancing teacher; a yoga instructor; and a divorce investigator. She is studying to become a certified graphologist (handwriting analyst). She is married and the mother of three teenagers.

ANNE PENNEBAKER is thirteen years old and lives in Fort Worth, Texas. She is an honor student at Saint Andrews Catholic School. She enjoys writing, dancing, playing basketball, and spending time with her friends, and is a member of the National Junior Honor Society. She has loved writing ever since she was young. Her story "Getting Over Him" is her first story to be published.

KATHLEEN PIMENTEL is a retired high school French teacher married to a retired university German professor. In order to keep up their language skills and cultural knowledge, and for any other imaginable excuse, they travel to Europe as often as possible. They love classical music and have attended the ten-day Wagner opera festival in Beyreuth, Germany, four times. She also enjoys golf, taking cooking lessons (far more than the actual cooking), skiing, and sitting in her backyard with friends and her husband, Ray. After a career of reading and correcting her students' compositions, she is delighted to be writing herself.

FELICE R. PRAGER is a freelance writer from Scottsdale, Arizona. Her work has appeared in international, national, and local publications, as well as many e-zines. FelPrager@aol.com. http://www.writefunny.com

MARGARET C. PRICE has written novels, screenplays, and stage plays. A graduate of Northwestern University in speech and the University of Kentucky College of Law, she has acted with Actors Theatre of Louisville and advocated children's rights as an attorney. A member of the Writers Guild, she studied film at the American Film Institute and the University of London. She recently placed second in the National Practical Paradox Screen Play Competition with her screenplay *Looking for Mrs. Santa Claus*. She lives in Lexington, Kentucky, with her husband, Gary, and their three daughters, Meredith, Julie, and Katie. (606) 263-8131

LISA SANDERS is a stay-at-home mom to two preschoolers, Torri and Teague. She says her husband, Rich, is her best friend, boyfriend, and one true love. Although she no longer stands in front of a classroom, this former teacher believes she has "chalk dust on the sleeve of her soul." A nationally published freelance writer, she specializes in family and education articles. Samples of her work can be viewed at her Web site, www.Joy-Writer.com. Lisa@Joy-Writer.com

KELLY SCHEUFLER is a San Diego–based writer, foster child advocate, and mother of three. She has published several articles about peace activists as well as personal essays. She is currently gathering stories from her relatives and aspires to put together a book chronicling her family's ancestors. Scheufler@email.msn.com

SHELLEY SIGMAN is a freelance writer and photographer who, after twenty-one years heading her own landscape design company, traded her T-square for the tools of writing. She is an entertainment reporter for the *Main Line Times* in suburban Philadelphia and former lifestyle feature writer and restaurant columnist for Gannett Newspapers. She's had articles, humor, and fiction featured in the *Chicago Tribune, Philadelphia's Exponent, Green's Magazine,* and *Reader's Break.* siggie@enter.net

ALAINA SMITH is a writer. Although her jobs have included newspaper editor, training coordinator, and office manager, fiction writing will always be her primary passion. Working on her novel and composing short stories keep her busy, and her loving and supportive husband, Frank, keeps her inspired. writersmith@yahoo.com

SHEILA STEPHENS is an international award–winning poet, writing teacher, columnist, and speaker who enjoys helping people build their lives "from the inside out." To her, self-esteem is a spiritual journey of accepting the seed of love that divine spirit places in each heart. She has just completed *Walking with the Flowers: 50 Weeks of Quiet Meditations for a Woman's Busy World.* Her professional services include creativity coaching; personalized correspondence writing classes (available worldwide); and "Walking with the Flowers" Seminars. joywriters@hotmail.com

SUSAN B. TOWNSEND is a writer and stay-at-home mother to five children ranging in ages from three to sixteen. Transplanted four years ago from the west coast of Canada, she and her husband, Tom, live on a 300-acre farm in southeastern Virginia with their children and a multitude of pets. She is at work on her first novel. (804) 834-2245. monitor@visi.net

GAYLE TRENT is the author of *Photo Finish,* a romantic suspense novel published by Neighborhood Press, and of *Mama Liked Blue,* a children's book published by Kudlicka Publishing. She also enjoys writing nonfiction articles such as "How to Write a Business Plan" and "Valuing Your Small Business," in "Venture Portfolio" (online); "Summer Boredom Busters," in "The Dollar Stretcher" newsletter; and "Self-Promotion for the Emerging Writer," for Writing-World.com. In addition, she has her own newsletter, "Writing up a Storm." http://hometown.aol.com/gayletrent/myhomepage/profile.html

MARY H. WU is a nineteen-year-old Manhattanville College sophomore. She has been writing since she was ten years old and has been published in *TeenInk*. She is currently working on a novel and her biggest goal is getting the novel published. Besides writing, she enjoys America Online, listening to music, traveling, and doing calligraphy. (914) 747-3849. LiLFortuneCookie@aol.com

BETH ZIEMNIK is a recent graduate of John Carroll University and is currently on a quest to find her passion in life. Along this journey she cherishes time spent with family, friends, and every individual who influences her life. She has a special place in her heart for youth and has volunteered at the community center of Big Ugly, West Virginia, and the farm town of Immokalee, Florida. For seven months she led retreats for high-school students in Milford, Ohio, at a Jesuit retreat house. A communications major, she enjoys creative writing and public speaking and one day hopes to work in a nonprofit organization's special events department. If she could pick any job in the world, she would love to be a motivational speaker. bethaz@aol.com

ACKNOWLEDGMENTS

A very warm thank-you to those of you who shared your true, poignant stories in *Chocolate for a Teen's Spirit*. Because of you, young women around the world will be inspired and encouraged to lead outrageously fulfilling and spirit-filled lives.

As always, my heartfelt thanks goes to my editor, Caroline Sutton, for her expertise, encouragement, and taste for *Chocolate*. My gratitude to all of you at Fireside / Simon & Schuster, who have made the *Chocolate* series so special: Mark Gompertz, Trish Todd, Christine Lloreda, Nicole Diamond, Lisa Sciambra, Cherlynne Lee, Julie Sanders, Laura Oppenheimer, Marie Floria, and so many more.

I send kudos to my marvelous agent, Peter Miller. His devoted, tireless energy to *Chocolate* has warmed my spirit and the spirit of readers around the globe. And a special thank-you goes to his energetic staff as well.

Closer to home, my deep appreciation to Jan Richardson and Tamara Johnson, who daily get a taste of *Chocolate* as they assist me and all the *Chocolate* sisters. And a very special nod goes to my editing pals, Burky Achilles and Sheila Stephens.

Last, but never least, much love to my husband, family, and friends—for they have all made *Chocolate* a special part of their lives.

ABOUT THE AUTHOR

Kay Allenbaugh is the author of *Chocolate for a Woman's Soul, Chocolate for a Woman's Heart, Chocolate for a Lover's Heart, Chocolate for a Mother's Heart, Chocolate for a Woman's Spirit, Chocolate for a Teen's Soul, Chocolate for a Woman's Blessings, Chocolate for a Teen's Heart,* and *Chocolate for a Woman's Dreams.* She resides with her husband, Eric Allenbaugh (author of *Wake-Up Calls: You Don't Have to Sleepwalk Through Your Life, Love or Career*), in Lake Oswego, Oregon.